Turn to God

Rejoice in Hope

Turn to God
Rejoice in Hope

Bible Studies-Meditations-Liturgical Aids

WCC Publications, Geneva

Cover design: Edwin Hassink/WCC

ISBN 2-8254-1185-X

Printed in Switzerland

Contents

Introduction

The World Council of Churches

This book is offered to Christians and the churches in preparation for the eighth assembly of the World Council of Churches to be held in Harare, Zimbabwe, in September 1998. According to its Basis, the World Council of Churches (WCC) is "a fellowship of churches which confess the Lord Jesus Christ as God and Saviour according to the Scriptures and therefore seek to fulfil together their common calling to the glory of the one God, Father, Son and Holy Spirit".

Together this fellowship of churches seeks to fulfil a *common vocation*. Rooted in and empowered by the search for Christian unity, and linking the churches in common witness, mission, service and renewal, this vocation is undertaken in obedience to Christ's prayer "that they may be one... that the world may believe" (John 17:21).

The WCC was founded in 1948 by delegates from 147 churches who assembled in Amsterdam. Its roots were in two movements which had been working since the early 20th century to overcome the divisions in doctrine and sacramental practice among churches (Faith and Order) and to promote common action in areas of Christian witness and service (Life and Work). Later, two other major Christian movements merged with the WCC as well: the International Missionary Council in 1961 and the World Council of Christian Education in 1971.

In mid-1996 WCC includes some 330 member churches, Protestant and Orthodox, from all regions of the world. As a fellowship of churches the WCC promotes the common confession of faith and the common life, reflection and action of its members, but has itself no legislative authority. There are extensive contacts with the Roman

Catholic Church, which is, however, not a member of the WCC. In addition, there are increasing contacts with evangelical and Pentecostal churches. The WCC works, wherever appropriate, in cooperation with national and regional ecumenical organizations, confessional bodies and other ecumenical groups.

The eighth assembly

Like its predecessors, the eighth assembly will bring together official delegates from WCC member churches, representatives of other churches, guests, advisors, staff, stewards and visitors. The delegates have three basic constitutional responsibilities: to review the work done by the WCC since the previous assembly in Canberra, Australia, in 1991; to set out the WCC's programmatic priorities for the period until the next assembly; and to elect those who will govern the WCC in the next period. But the life of the assembly will be enriched and broadened by acts of common worship, encounters with the scriptures and the chance for participants to share testimonies and life stories with other Christians who are seeking, in their own situations all around the world, to live out the gospel message today. An extensive media operation will in turn work to disseminate the decisions and experiences of the assembly to all parts of the world.

In addition, several elements will come together at this assembly, making it certainly a decisive moment, and possibly a decisive turning-point, in the churches' ecumenical journey. There will be celebrations to mark the year 1998 as the 50th anniversary of the founding of the WCC. A process is now underway to take account of the momentous changes in the churches, the ecumenical movement and the world since 1948, and to identify a new "common understanding and vision" of the WCC. This common understanding and vision will be celebrated at the assembly in a solemn and festive act of liturgical appropriation. And there will be the chance for participants, including church leaders, to offer their commitment to a fresh ecumenical vision for the future.

The number of participants who attend an assembly is necessarily limited; but Christians everywhere can be part of the assembly process, both before and after the gathering itself. This can happen through meetings with assembly delegates or other participants, both before and after the event, for discussion of the concerns and issues considered by the assembly. In particular, it can happen through using the material in this book, either within your own church or Christian group or in an ecumenical setting. Some suggestions for using the various parts of this book are given below.

For further information about the assembly or the WCC Common Understanding and Vision process, please write to the WCC Assembly Office in Geneva, Switzerland or (for residents of North America) the WCC Office in New York.

The assembly theme

The assembly theme "Turn to God — Rejoice in Hope" expresses the threefold structure of Christian faith and life: God turns to us in grace; we respond in faith, acting in love; and we anticipate the coming, final fullness of God's presence in all of creation. These three elements — memory, praxis (putting faith into action) and hope — are distinct but inseparable moments in the life of faith. They are grounded in God's unshakable fidelity, Christ's saving acts and the Spirit's powerful presence. They remind us of the threefold nature of the church as a community of memory and interpretation, a community of love in action, and a community of hope.

The theme calls us to *turn to God*, the God who has first turned to us in love and grace. Through remembering God's fidelity and through celebrating, in acts of worship, God's liberating acts in history and in the whole of creation, we affirm our place among God's people. We proclaim God's presence and affirm that the reign of God has drawn near, that God's promises are being fulfilled. In joyful response we turn to God, discovering ourselves and our true humanity in the process. It is first a turning to God, and away from all idols — all the false values and securities which claim us today; it is also a turning to our neighbours, in loving kindness and humble service; and it is a turning which seeks to do justice to others and to the whole of God's creation.

The theme calls us to *rejoice in hope*. It is a radical hope, a hope based not in human possibilities but in God's faithfulness and mighty deeds. In raising Jesus to new life, God affirms the way of the cross, the power of Christ's self-offering love. It is an inclusive hope, one which insists that all are brought within the scope of God's love and care. Such a hope is inspired by the vision of the Trinity as a community of mutual sharing and love, one in which domination has no place. Through the outpouring of the Holy Spirit, the promised age has already entered history, but not yet in its fullness; the signs of the kingdom are manifest, but we still pray "Your kingdom come" (Matt. 6:10). Thus our hope is rooted in God's promise finally to gather up all things in Christ: we hope, finally, for the transformation of humanity and of the whole creation.

Many of these notions come together in the tradition of the "jubilee year". This calls for the restoration of relationship between God's people and God, thus enabling and empowering the restoration of community among God's people. Strikingly, this is made visible in the community's social and economic life: for example, through the restoration of property and the exercise of justice for the oppressed (Lev. 25:8-17, 39-43). Such a vision is a powerful source of hope. These concerns are prominent in the ministry of Jesus, for example through his proclamation of the inbreaking of the "year of the Lord's favour" (Luke 4:16-21), and in the Lord's Prayer (Matt. 6:12; Luke 11:4).

About this book

Preparation for WCC assemblies has traditionally focussed on Bible studies on the theme. While this method has been successful and well received, there are situations in which other types of preparatory material would be more useful for individuals, churches or Christian groups. For example, in contexts of preaching and teaching, sermon notes or theological reflections on the theme might be especially helpful. Some churches, not so familiar with this form of Bible study, would find material relating to a liturgical context, and the liturgical calendar, more helpful. In short, a varied set of preparatory materials, approaching the theme from different perspectives and using different educational methods, would serve a wider constituency and encourage a more comprehensive preparation of the churches for the eighth assembly.

This book, therefore, represents a new approach to the material: *it contains not one but three distinct types of material*. These are not mutually exclusive, nor are they the same material presented in three different formats. While all the material is related to the assembly theme, the content (for example, the biblical texts cited) is sufficiently varied that more than one of the types of material could be used within the same church or Christian community.

The three sets of preparatory material are set out in the three following sections of this book. Each section is introduced by an explanatory note; we indicate here the key concept behind each approach, and the main topics covered.

Bible studies

These seven Bible studies, in a lively traditional format, focus on matters which are likely to be central to the reflection on the theme at the assembly. These are addressed under the following headings:

1. "For such a time": Isaiah 1:2-17; 1 John 1:1-4
2. "The year of the Lord's favour" – Jubilee: Leviticus 25:8-17. 39-43; Luke 4:16-21
3. "We, who are many, are one body": 1 Corinthians 12:12-31
4. "God shows no partiality": Galatians 3:26-28; Acts 11:1-18
5. "Bear one another's burdens": John 13:1-35; Genesis 18:1-15; Galatians 6:1-10
6. "A witness between the generations": Joshua 22:10-29; Deuteronomy 6:20-25; 2 Timothy 1:1-7
7. "A cloud of witnesses": Hebrews 11:1-3, 11:39-12:2

Meditations

These six meditations, bringing biblical texts into relation with personal experiences, cover various aspects of the theme as follows:

1. Turning to the living God
2. The God to whom we turn
3. Marks of a life turned to God
4. Turning to a living hope
5. Rejoicing in hope
6. The hope of the nations

Liturgical resources

These five theme-related reflections, on biblical texts assigned in the Orthodox tradition for Sundays of the Lenten period, include liturgical material. This section is arranged under the following headings:

1. The great return: recognition of sin, reconciliation: Isaiah 1:4; Luke 15:11-32
2. Participation in the joy of the Lord's presence: Exodus 40:34-36; John 1:44-52
3. Messengers of hope: Isaiah 8:16-18; Matt. 25:31-46
4. Call to true worship: Psalm 50; John 12:1-18
5. Cross, resurrection, Pentecost – the hope: Isaiah 52:13; Mark 8:34-39

The preparation and use of this book

This book is the fruit of a long process involving many persons from around the world. The names of those who have been involved are listed in the acknowledgments on page 101. We are grateful to all those who have contributed material, and we offer special thanks to the editors of each of the sections.

The material in this book is intended for use in the churches and Christian communities. Individuals, pastors, group leaders, educators, and editors are invited to use or adapt one or more sections of the material according to their local needs and circumstances. We urge you to be as practical and concrete in your approach as possible, relating the material to the situation of those who use it. Should you photocopy or otherwise reproduce parts of the text for distribution to members of a study group, we ask that you acknowledge the source of the material you use.

As an additional resource the World Council of Churches, in cooperation with the United Bible Societies, is developing a "Scripture Portion", a booklet of biblical texts which will bring together the text of most of the scripture passages referred to in the present book, as well as a few others, in a form convenient for study and reflection. The booklet is expected to be ready in early 1997 and will be distributed in each country by the local Bible Society working in cooperation with the churches.

We pray that you will find this material helpful in your preparation for the eighth assembly of the World Council of Churches, and in your own spiritual life. May it strengthen and encourage you and your own Christian community in your reflection — and action — on the theme "Turn to God — Rejoice in Hope".

PART I

Bible Studies

Introductory Note

The format, length and content of these seven Bible studies, for which input has come from all the continents where the member churches of the World Council of Churches are living out their Christian witness, is not uniform. Each group that undertakes one or more of these studies will have to decide how best to use the time available for reading and talking about the biblical text, following the suggestions for discussion at the end of each study and taking up concerns which members of the group have felt and articulated during this time. The group may wish to plan further study and action before proceeding to the following studies — or it may choose to return to it later.

As with any serious encounter with the Bible, more is at stake here than simply improving our intellectual understanding of an ancient text. These studies may even lead to a fundamental shift in the understanding of our faith in terms of the biblical message. And they are certainly intended to inspire personal and collective commitments and actions. Before closing each session, the group may want to return to the opening stories provided in the material, as well as other stories offered by the participants, and deal with the questions that these stories evoke.

In addition to studying the Bible, this is a chance to take time to pray together and to move from reading the text into some appropriate actions that illustrate an obedient readiness to live out God's words. May the Spirit of God nurture the hope which is the inseparable companion of our faith.

"For Such a Time"

Isaiah 1:2-17 — 1 John 1:1-4

Esther's time. It is difficult to confront a time of crisis in isolation. "For just such a time" Esther was called to speak and to bring relief and deliverance to her people (Esther 4:14). But she did not do that alone. Esther needed the help of Mordecai and the community: "Go, gather all the Jews to be found in Susa, and hold a fast on my behalf" (v.16). She prepared herself well too: "I and my maids will also fast as you do." We can imagine that the memory of the great courage of Vashti (Esther 1:10-22) helped her to intercede for her people.

The inspiration of Esther's life invites us to pay attention to our own times. We are living a very special time today. There are many elements that make it different and unique, but the most meaningful motif is that it is the time of our own life. It is the time God has given us as a precious gift: "For everything there is a season, and a time for every matter under heaven" (Eccl. 3:1).

For a long time our planet was divided by a vertical line — on one side the West, on the other the East. The cold war scarred us. We also saw a horizontal line that divided the rich Northern countries from the poor Southern ones. These two lines came together in the form of a cross over our planet. They symbolized the suffering of the people.

A time of human suffering can be a time of pain, agony, confusion and even despair, but more often than not it is also a time of expectation, a time of hope. Today powerful forces have decreed the end of the political lines separating East and West and have assured us that the market economy will eradicate all other dividing lines. "Globalization" is presented as the answer to our expectation, the source of our hope.

The reality is that people at the local level all over the world are feeling more and more the invisible forces that divide us. They see a particular way of life invading their daily lives, threatening their jobs, making the burden of their work heavier, especially for women and children. Our time is still a time of divisions, now made visible in the power of silver and gold. From east to west, north to south, the haves and have-nots continue to travel in opposite directions. There is insecurity throughout our lands and the lines of division radiate through the earth like ink on blotting-paper.

More than ever we are called in "just such a time" to respond to the voices of those who suffer from the inhuman ways of life imposed on them. At such a time we turn to the Bible to ask what God is saying *to* our times and *through* our times. Where is God in all of this? Who has seen or heard or felt God in our times? For such a time as this we turn to God to listen and to heed. In this study we seek to learn from Isaiah 1:2-17 and 1 John 1:1-4.

Text and context

Isaiah 1:2-17. There were times when war was a means of achieving social transformation. Today we recognize that wars are instruments only of death. The prophet Isaiah portrays the disastrous results of war: "Your country lies desolate, your cities are burned with fire; in your very presence aliens devour your land…" (1:7). The prophet called his people to turn to God, for they were deserting their faith in the God of life: "Ah, sinful nation…, who have forsaken the Lord, who have despised the Holy One of Israel, who are utterly estranged!" (v.4).

At the time Isaiah 1 was written, eight centuries before the birth of Jesus Christ, the nations east of the Mediterranean and around what we now call the Persian Gulf were living through a period of crisis and war. Empires and kingdoms were in the throes of change, and war was the instrument of this change. It was a time of anxiety and transition. In 742 B.C., Assyria invaded Israel. The rulers of Judah, just to the south, became nervous and began to look for allies to protect them against Assyria. Isaiah prophesies this impending threat and explains the reason for it (vv.4-6). He saw this search for political alliances as further evidence of the people's lack of faith in Yahweh and their myopia concerning God's purposes.

Isaiah 1:2-17 shows us God, with a woman's diligence, setting about the work of retrieving God's people. Through the prophets, God seeks to turn the people from evil (v.18). What God asks is repentance, not debilitating self-pity nor ostentatious worship nor impressive statements in which we try to assert and establish that we are a people without acknowledging our guilt and alienation from God.

Formal worship is due to God as an expression of our reverence for God, but it cannot supersede or replace our human relations. In fact, it is nullified and becomes positively irksome to God if we make it a substitute for doing justice and helping the oppressed (vv.10-17). The message of the prophet was that the political and social crises were the result of religious disloyalty, social injustice, greed, corruption and attachment to material things. The people's self-indulgence and pride have so clouded their vision that they can no longer discern God's presence and activity. Isaiah pours condemnation on the visionless and corrupt leaders, the perpetrators of injustice. The prophet's message echoes the meaning of his own name — "Yahweh will deliver; Yahweh is salvation". God's main concern, declares the prophet, is that human beings should resemble the source of their being. They should imitate God. Like Amos (5:1-24), Hosea (6:6; 8:11-14), Micah (6:6-8) and Jeremiah (7:22-23), Isaiah portrays God as compassionate, full of goodness, truth and justice.

1 John 1:1-10. The three letters of 1 John, 2 John and 3 John address conflict within the church. During the initial period of the Christian church when these letters were written, theology was in a very fluid stage, and doctrine was being forged through the many conflicts and controversies that rocked the churches.

We can see the internal doctrinal crisis very clearly in the first letter of John (ch. 2). The main issues in 1 John arise out of differing opinions about living in fellowship and love with one another (2:9-11) and about the humanity of Jesus (4:2-3). The affirmation of Christ's incarnation (4:2) shows us the tangibility of God's presence in the world. We must read this verse alongside 3:16ff., where we are invited to accept our common ethical responsibility towards others and relate words and actions in a meaningful way.

The imagery of light and darkness used in 1:5-7 has become problematic because it has been read with racial connotations to suggest somehow that to have a dark skin is to be evil and a light skin means goodness. It goes without saying that nothing could be further from the truth. Sin befriends all human beings, not just those of one race or gender. Knowing to fear and avoid evil, rather than what is dark, is a human responsibility that falls on everyone. This letter, however, was written within a culture that made the opposition of darkness and light represent the antagonism between truth and falsehood, evil and goodness. Surely it is not beyond our imagination to find other language in our times to distinguish between what is in tune with the nature of God and what is not.

The letter of 1 John tries to make a clear distinction between what unites us with Christ and what alienates us from Christ (2:3-6). Our religious codes and our prayers must cohere (1:5-8). Failure in this area is what sin is about.

Fellowship, love and truth are three major emphases in the letter (1:3-4). In order to talk about fellowship, the writer uses family language. Through family language the relationship between Jesus and God is established (2:22-24). Being in fellowship is about living in community with others. Community is central to this letter; and to refer to the members of the community the author uses such terms of endearment as "beloved" (2:7), "(my) little children" (2:1; 3:7), "children of God" (3:1; 5:2).

The fellowship mentioned in 1:3, with all its connotations, is the truth, which is not confined to the conventional institutional church but extended to the entire world (3:11-23). The central ethical demand flowing out of this fellowship is "that we should love one another" (3:11). The sharing of love is the mark of fellowship and the mark of humanity. That humanity leads to the understanding of the humanity of Jesus and the love of God: "those who love God must love their brothers and sisters also" (4:21; cf. 2:9-11; 4:11-12).

Here we find a close connection with the prophetic message (Isaiah 1:16-17) of costly commitment. At the same time, 1 John is a clear invitation to turn to God (1:9-10) as the God of love, faithfulness and forgiveness (4:7-21). The important principle of this union with the Christian community, with Christ and with God is faith and love.

Suggestions for discussion

1. Esther was a messenger of hope in her time and place. Who are the messengers of hope in your time and place?

2. What is your understanding and local experience of "globalization"?
3. Like the days when the epistle of 1 John was written, our times are not free from conflicts. What conflicts occupy your community and church? What are the "invisible lines" of division spreading within your community? What practical responses might the community plan in the face of those conflicts?
4. What are the sins which we are not confessing today as churches or as members of a particular community? How could we "turn to God" in our present situation? What is the role of our worship in this? How can we relate worship to our daily life? Look at Isaiah 1:11-17 as a source of inspiration for your analysis.

"The Year of the Lord's Favour": Jubilee

Leviticus 25:8-17, 39-43 — Luke 4:16-21

"It could happen to anyone..." It was Sunday morning. We arrived early at our small church. It was communion Sunday, a day of expectation and hope. We were ready to begin our liturgy when Eric, the president of the congregation, arrived. We could see the signs of sadness and depression in his eyes as he told us what had happened to him the previous Friday.

Eric is 57 years old, with three children, one of them only 12. For more than 20 years he has worked in a factory that makes sewing machines, living in relative security. Then on Friday at 11 a.m. the factory owner had called 147 workers together and told them that their contracts would end at 5 p.m. the same day. The factory was bankrupt.

Holy communion had a very special meaning for us on that Sunday morning. "This is my body which is for you... This cup is the new covenant in my blood." In Christ we shared Eric's suffering. But others in the congregation said, "This could happen to any of us today, tomorrow, next week." In some parts of the world unemployment and underemployment now affect 30, 50 or even 70 percent of the population, producing unprecedented poverty and marginalization. What had happened to Eric reminded us that the threat of layoffs is increasing everywhere, creating new levels of stress and insecurity.

We held hands during the last hymn, which united us in fellowship and love: "The peace of the resurrected Christ be with all of us, today and forever." But some of us went home asking ourselves whether the God of the Bible requires more than prayer and sympathy for times like this.

Buried and resurrected. *Rosangela is part of a group of Brazilian farmers who had no land of their own and so joined together to set up* *a squatter community on an hacienda that belonged to the government, near the city of Santo Augusto, in the state of Rio Grande do Sul. It wasn't long before the police threw them off the land. With support from several churches and other people of good will, the group camped for nine months by the side of a highway. Through continuous political pressure on the government, they finally obtained permission to occupy an abandoned hacienda that the government had expropriated in Erval Seco.*

In Rosangela's words, "We were buried in Santo Augusto and resurrected in Erval Seco!" With several harvests behind her, she is now managing to support her family. And when this new community started an alternative school on the property, Rosangela took courses and became a teacher for the children of the group.

Rosangela's experience raises basic questions, particularly for people of faith, about the rights of the landless and justice for people whom our local and global economy push to the edges of society.

Text and context

The Bible has far more to say about God's will for economic life than most of us realize. And those teachings are presented as "spiritual" issues, not just "material" concerns. We know of course that God liberated the Hebrew people from slavery in Egypt and brought them to the Promised Land so that they might be God's people and live according to God's commandments. Leviticus 25 tells us how they were to order their social-economic-spiritual life, and it offers fundamental challenges for us today.

Before going into the details of this chapter, we should briefly consider its background and context. This material was probably put together when the remaining tribes of Israel were returning from exile (6th century B.C.), but its roots go back to the founding of their nation (13th century B.C.) and it reflects the concerns of the prophets during the monarchy (11th to 6th centuries B.C.). The chapter summarizes God's commandments regarding the sabbath year (every 7 years) and the jubilee year (every 50 years). Much of the focus is on ownership of the land, which was the primary source of economic life, social life and even family and personal life.

It is easy to see that mandates for the sabbath year and the jubilee year are addressed to one of the most burning problems of ancient

Israel, of Jesus' day and even of our own generation. The land, like other resources for economic life, tends to fall into the hands of a few who become rich, and the majority become poor. In ancient times most of the people lived off the land. When their crops failed, they went into debt; and if they were unable to pay back their debt (often with very high interest), they lost their land. Then they became sharecroppers, day-labourers or even slaves. They might eventually be forced into begging, prostitution and other "unclean" work, as their families faced severe undernourishment and disease and finally death.

The teachings about the sabbath year and jubilee year (compare Deuteronomy 15:1-18) are a direct and revolutionary (though non-violent) response to that social and economic problem, which at times became the central issue in Israel's life and a central concern of Israel's God.

> Ask yourselves if the problem of land ownership, debts and employment (including slavery) in ancient agrarian societies is clear to all. Explore what Leviticus 25 and Deuteronomy 15:1-18 disclose about God's will regarding the accumulation of land, debts, slavery and the preservation of the land, and draw comparisons with modern societies. To facilitate this, the group may be divided into subgroups, each assigned to prepare and share a summary of one of the paragraphs in these two passages.

It is important to note how directly these mandates are related to Israel's faith. The jubilee was to be proclaimed on the Day of Atonement (*Yom Kippur*), the most sacred day of the year. On that day and only on that day the high priest entered the Holy of Holies to offer sacrifices for the cleansing of the temple, the priesthood and the people; and a goat was sent into the desert to symbolize the expulsion of their sins. The fulfilment of the jubilee mandates was thus seen as necessary for communion with God. Furthermore, these mandates themselves are based on the fundamental beliefs of Israel.

The jubilee and sabbath year mandates are not arbitrary or isolated teachings. They express the fundamental logic of God's intervention in human and cosmic history. The God of the Exodus, who delivered the Hebrew people out of slavery in Egypt into a "land flowing with milk and honey", had every right to expect them to resist and reverse the very human but sinful tendencies towards wealth and poverty, domination and alienation. God's justice, which is based on God's saving grace, demands fullness of life for all the people.

This concern was expressed repeatedly by the Old Testament prophets. In Isaiah 61:1-2a (compare Isa. 58:6) we find a direct reference to the jubilee year as "the year of the Lord's favour". That passage was in turn used by Jesus to explain the central concern of his ministry (Luke 4:16-31). Several of the prophets were so vehement about God's demand for justice that they called into question the very worship of Israel and foretold the destruction of the temple. In the same way Jesus confronted the religious establishment of his time, which was linked with the wealthy landholders, the temple-state and the Roman empire.

In fulfilment of the jubilee mandates Jesus brought good news to the poor as the breaking in of God's reign, as the release of those in prison (most of whom were there because of debts), as recovery of sight to the blind and healing for all kinds of diseases, as liberation of the oppressed. He taught that God's reign would comfort those who mourn, give land back to the meek and fill the hungry with justice. Not only did he heal the sick, but he broke the taboos that marginalized people, above all the unclean, the sinners, women and children, and he gave them first priority in God's reign. To do this he had to challenge the guardians of the social, economic, political and religious system, first the scribes and Pharisees, later the Herodians and the Sadducees, finally the high priests.

Jesus taught his disciples to pray for the coming of God's reign, to forgive debts, to serve one another with humility and to be ready to give their lives as he was bound to do.

Giving examples from your knowledge of the gospels, discuss how Jesus carried out the general concerns of the jubilee in very concrete ways. Then give examples from Acts and the New Testament epistles of how the early church also tried to fulfil the jubilee mandates. Finally, give some examples of jubilee experiences through the history of the church up to the present.

Having considered these important biblical teachings, we must ask ourselves how faithful we are to God's commandments as they are expressed in terms of the jubilee and sabbath year. How can *we* bring good news to the poor, release to prisoners, sight to the blind, liberation to the oppressed? We must bring these mandates down to our daily lives in concrete ways, remembering that Jesus, through small acts of healing and caring and even by disobeying legalistic regulations, was breaking down the walls of oppression and bringing in God's reign.

At the same time we must relate the central mandates of Leviticus 25 and Deuteronomy 15:1-18 to the central crises of our time. And we must pray for the coming of God's reign in terms of the biblical jubilee in response to the struggles of all God's people for fullness of life.

Suggestions for discussion

1. Take a few moments to meditate on the two stories at the beginning of this study. What would it be like to find yourselves in such a situation? Then share your own stories about economic insecurity, poverty and marginalization. What is your local church teaching and doing about these realities?
2. What does it mean to give "rest to the land" (Lev. 25:5)? Can this be applied today to an ecosystem about to collapse, leading to planetary death?
3. In your community how does the increasing concentration in fewer hands of the resources necessary to participate in the economy, society and life as a whole affect the people? What are some creative ways of reallocating available resources for the life and well-being of all God's people and all of creation?
4. What does it mean today to free the slaves? Could this call for liberation be applied to peasants and workers at all levels who are subject without appeal to the "invisible hand" of the market and thus permanently exposed to the threat of layoff, which can mean economic death?
5. The debts which many poor countries owe to foreign banks, governments and financial institutions are now being used to enforce their submission to outside economic powers, who are requiring them to dismantle social welfare systems to the point of bringing about what some call ungovernability, and others refer to as social explosion. How do these "jubilee" texts speak to this situation?

"We, Who Are Many, Are One Body"
1 Corinthians 12:12-31

Are some "more equal"? *I cannot accept this injustice. Just because we are a minority church, we are denied all privileges. Our pastors do not receive from the state the pay to which they — just as the clergy of the majority church — are entitled. Nor do we receive help for the maintenance of our church buildings. Most of the government leaders come from the dominant church. Yet not even the Christian believers in that church are willing to support us and speak up about our needs. They see any possible gain for us as taking away their privileges. How can we claim together to be "one body"? This is really very difficult for me to come to terms with.*

To be treated normally. *People's attitudes towards someone in a wheelchair can be very annoying and upsetting. Shopping on a Saturday can become a nightmare. People stand and stare at me or they give me funny looks. People never talk to you; they talk to whoever is pushing you. People think, just because you can't walk, you can't talk either. I don't know why they think this, but they do and it is very annoying. I would like to be treated normally, like everyone else, and one of my ambitions is to be able to go from one end of the street to the other without one person turning around to look at me* (from Heather Jones, in *What It Is Like To Be Me*, ed. Helen Exley, New York, Friendship Press, 1984, p.12).

Text and context

While some of us live in cultures which emphasize individual independence and achievement, others have a more corporate under-standing of identity in which the primary responsibility is to the group and individual achievements may even be seen as divisive and a potential fragmentation of the whole. The image of the Christian community as the Body of Christ, like many of the biblical images, is organic and relational. It conveys a strong sense of interdependence and implies an intrinsic potential for growth. Even in some other biblical images of the community which are at first glance stable and static, like that of a building or a house, disturbing elements indicating mobility are introduced.

Using images can be an instructive way to communicate. But the point of an image is not just to illustrate something already well-known. The most effective images slightly disorient our conventional ways of understanding. What is realistic and what is unusual, almost unimaginable, are woven together. Images help us to imagine what is otherwise beyond the capacity of language to describe, what does not fully correspond to any reality we have ever experienced. In theological terms one could say that this is the "eschatological dimension" of language.

At the same time, biblical images of communion also reflect structures of society and patterns of culture from their time of origin. Many of these structures were patriarchal and oppressive; and such images have also been used to maintain and even reinforce patterns of domination in church and society. One example is the model of the household. Many women today have difficulties perceiving the community of faith in "household" categories.

Is there any way to maintain the concern for communion in such images while dismantling their reflection of an unjust social system? Is it possible to renew such images from alternative experiences in other cultures? How do we develop a fair balance of power, true reciprocity and inclusivity, so that interdependence is not perverted into constantly new forms of exploitation? How may reconciliation happen without the victim paying the cost? How do we taste and glimpse in our lives on earth the reign of God?

The Christian community in Corinth at the time of Paul was threatened by severe divisions, both social and theological, which were about to tear them apart as a community. From Paul's first letter to them, it seems that the community was divided into different parties, and from chapter 12 on Paul addresses the tensions which the various spiritual gifts or charisms had caused in the congregation. Apparently some people considered speaking in tongues and prophesying to be more direct manifestations of the Spirit than other charisms. They therefore regarded themselves as more important than others.

In this situation of division and conflict Paul calls for unity by explaining how their partaking in the same divine gifts creates a koinonia — a fellowship or communion — among themselves. All spiritual gifts, in all their diversity, come from one and the same source; and so they have meaning only if they serve a common purpose.

To explain how these different gifts belong together and work together, Paul uses the image of a living organism in which every part has its own task and at the same time is nothing without the others. This image helps him to explain how closely interrelated are variety and oneness, the particular and the universal. The image Paul takes is that of a human body. This body is one but has many members, and "all the members, though many, are one body" (v.12). The interdependence of the members of the body makes each member in its specific function important. No matter how insignificant and subordinate it may feel or seem, even the most humble part is indispensable and has an effect on the totality. Diversity and differentiation need not compromise unity but rather promote it.

The use of the body as an image for a community was common in antiquity. Often it served the purpose of silencing people who were objecting to and revolting against unjust structures. Such people, it was argued, should be content to remain in their place. In other words, it was often used to support hierarchical and oppressive structures.

Paul develops the image of the body by identifying it as the body of Christ. The whole body belongs to Christ and none of the members can claim it for themselves. The believers are members of the body through baptism, having become one through the work of the Spirit independent of their race, gender and social status (Gal. 3:26-28). Partaking in the koinonia of the body of Christ is therefore different from being a member of a club which you pay to join and where you can choose the people with whom you are together.

In contrast to the common use of the image of the body, Paul tries to emphasize not only the importance of every member but especially the noble position of the weaker ones and those not normally considered to be honourable. The head is not more important than the arms or the toes or any other member. Indeed, the image as a whole is not interpreted in the direction of defining who is who; and in 1 Corinthians 12 the head is not even said to be Christ (as it is in the use of the body image in Ephesians 4).

Paul has in view especially those who doubt their spiritual gifts and who feel inferior to the charismatic leaders of the community. They are affirmed and encouraged. At the same time, he reminds those who might consider themselves in honourable positions that they are of no greater value than anyone else. The same Spirit distributes different gifts and it is necessary to be different, because "if the whole body were an eye, where would the hearing be?" (v.17). And a member without a body makes no sense. Every member needs the others, and in mutual respect and dependence on one another, each one finds an equilibrium. For indeed the scriptures require those who consider themselves strong or powerful to give up something of what they might wish to be for the sake of accommodating those who are weak (1 Cor. 8).

Accordingly, Paul states that "to each is given the manifestation of the Spirit for the common good" (12:7). He does not reject any of the spiritual gifts but introduces a criterion of discernment: whether the church — that is, the whole community — is being "built up" (14:5). This language echoes another image of the community: a building under constant construction, which Paul develops in 1 Corinthians 3: "You are... God's building... I laid a foundation, and someone else is building on it... For no one can lay any foundation other than the one that has been laid; that foundation is Jesus Christ" (vv.9-11). Here Paul is addressing the divisions that arose in Corinth because people were so dependent on their teachers that they formed separate groups, which dissociated themselves from each other. Paul understands his own work as interdependent with the work of other preachers and teachers. To preserve the unity of the community he emphasizes that its foundation in Christ cannot be divided. Furthermore, the element of process in the image of a building under construction carries with it a hope of eschatological fulfilment.

Central themes

The complementary images of the body and of building convey an understanding of the church as koinonia, as an inclusive community of men and women, young and old, of able-bodied people and people with disabling conditions.

• The *image of the building under construction* shows that koinonia, although given, still has to be realized. This realization is the calling of the church. Another biblical author develops the image of construction in an even more striking way by speaking of Christians as "living stones" (1 Pet. 2:5). As such they take an active part both in their own formation and in their function in the whole of the building. Thus Christians may be both builders and part of the building at the same time. This is the special quality of Christian koinonia, its fascination and its difficulty. To live together and for one another is not easy. You have to fit into the wall like a stone that has to be cut. But at the same time you are carried by other stones in the wall, which makes your task easier. And you are also the one who is responsible to find the right place for every stone. The progress of the construction depends on you. But you are not alone.

• The *image of the body* shows how koinonia works. It shows the interdependence and the dynamics within the community. The members of a body taken separately — without the rest of the body — are meaningless. Only in the context of the community of all the other members does the existence of one member make sense. Their sharing in the eucharistic celebration of the one bread which is the one body of Christ (1 Cor. 10:16) calls them together to be this one body in their diversity. This may also point further to their mission of being the body of Christ in the world. The image of the body of Christ tells us that we are Christ's hands, feet, ears, eyes. This call is embodied in the lives of those who live out their witness in entering into other people's pain, and finding Christ through that process. This is what Mother Teresa in Calcutta and many others elsewhere in the world are doing. It is also about being in solidarity with men forced into war, women baptized in the name of Christ yet denied opportunities to serve Christ in ordained ministry, children left in the streets to fend for themselves, persons with disabilities ignored and neglected.

Community therefore is being built through the use of our own bodies. With our bodies we take the risk of doing something constructive to bring change. Rosa Parks, an African American woman, is honoured today for refusing to move to a back seat on a bus in Montgomery, Alabama, and touching off a chain of events known as the civil rights movement in the USA. The changes in Eastern Europe

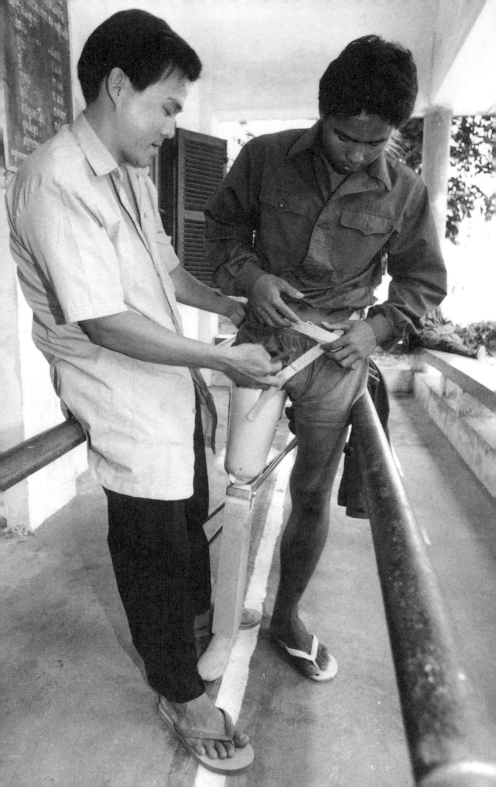

since 1989 have been the result of committed people willing to risk their lives, among other things by going into the streets to form human chains to say No to a system they no longer could live under. Nonviolent resistance in defence of people's lives and the environment by groups of women and men in India, the Philippines, Brazil, South Africa and other places are a matter of record. Events like these are happening in communities all over the world every day. Community is built where people are available for one another.

Koinonia is a complex concept of interdependence and exchange, diversity and unity. It is static and dynamic, complete and in process at the same time. Every community should review its own structures in a self-critical way to see if everyone has equal opportunity to contribute according to his or her gifts. This must happen in a constant process of dialogue, in which the awareness of the other becomes part of one's own identity. The idea that individuals or groups could live without others — and even think that they are superior human beings and that their version of the truth is the only possible way to salvation — is as absurd as the idea of a knee walking through the world without a leg or a body.

Suggestions for discussion

1. Take a close look at your home and community. Who does which jobs in the family, in the church and in the public sector? What kind of values are associated with these jobs?
2. What do you see as the major attitudes that most people have towards people with disabling conditions? Are there any programmes in your church or community designed to help everyone understand the needs and concerns of such persons?
3. Does your own experience as a member of a church suggest that the image of "one body" is a good image for the church? Why or why not? What other images for church or Christian community can you suggest?
4. What are your visions of community? What is the place of "individual freedom" within a community? What are your hopes for your community? For the ecumenical community?

BIBLE STUDY 4

"God Shows No Partiality"
Galatians 3:26-28 — Acts 11:1-18

A gift of sandals. In a village congregation in South India, some of the people attending the worship service one Sunday morning received a pair of sandals. The recipients were Dalits. In the past — but even today in villages in some parts of India — Dalits were not allowed to wear shoes. This prohibition has been imposed on them by others who refer to them offensively as "untouchables" and consider them worthy only of walking in the dust. So the sandals offered to these Dalits on this Sunday morning were like garlands offered to a visiting god.

The ties that bind. When a foreign visitor attended a wedding in the mid-1970s in what was then Yugoslavia, she marvelled at the deep sense of community evident at the dinner party after the church ceremony, as family and friends of the bride and groom joined in song after song from centuries past. They were sharing the bonds that had kept alive their sense of being a people even after decades of communist repression. Nearly 20 years later, it occurred to her that this very attachment to an ethnic tradition, so impressive at the wedding, with its enthusiastic songs celebrating vivid memories of heroic battles long ago, was now serving to fuel a bitter and bloody civil war.

Text and context

Early Christian teaching acknowledged that baptism brought an end to distinctions based on gender, culture, religion, ethnicity and social standing; and it is on the basis of baptism that Paul proclaims the unity of all Christians in Galatians 3:26-28: we have all been brought into God's family through faith in Jesus Christ. These verses incorporate a traditional baptismal formula which was probably used widely in the early church. Some have called the earliest church a "fellowship of equals" in which, as this text indicates, ethnic, economic and gender barriers were considered irrelevant for entrance into and inclusion in the group.

As the text itself goes on to make clear, the masculine usage "sons of God" (v.26; translated "children of God" by the New Revised Standard Version) in no way excludes women; rather, it is intended to underscore our oneness in Christ by connecting it with Jesus' own relationship to God as the Son. As people who have been baptized, Paul says, "you have clothed yourselves with Christ". We have been transformed; we have been shaped into Christ; we have taken up Christ's image; we are a new creation.

In three sharply worded phrases, Paul erases the divisions that separated people in the world of his day: "There is no longer Jew or Greek, there is no longer slave or free, there is no longer male and female."

"No longer Jew or Greek" recalls the fact that Christianity at first defined itself exclusively in ethnic terms, as a movement within Judaism. In Acts 11 we read about a radical change on this score, as Peter tells the church leaders in Jerusalem how his in-group mentality was shattered by an experience in the house of the Roman military officer Cornelius. Peter's message is clear: "God abolished all the differences between us! The Holy Spirit was poured out on that Gentile's household, just as on us at the beginning!" With the baptism of the family of Cornelius, the unity of the church suddenly became unity in diversity, embracing many different ethnic groups.

In distant Galatia, as in the church at Jerusalem, diversity provoked conflict over how to achieve unity. In his letter to the Galatians, Paul confronts those who wanted to impose their own categories on others. First he reminds the Galatian Christians that the Spirit has been powerfully manifested among them (compare Peter's similar argument in Acts 11:15). Then he recites the baptismal formula to crown his explanation that faith in God's grace as seen in Jesus Christ is the only requirement for full acceptance. Freed from all impositions, the diverse groups face only one imperative: to love and serve each other (5:13).

Yet ethnic divisions and conflicts continue to plague our world today. Racism is still a violent reality. Even in our churches, sisters and brothers experience discrimination. The Christian concept of the realm of God is one in which wholeness, justice, love, peace, equality and freedom are made manifest. By affirming the message of love, we communicate to those who may feel excluded — women, people living with disabling conditions, the poor, gay and lesbian people, the sick and the dying — that the God of Jesus Christ is God for all.

What insights does the letter to the Galatians offer to help us face up to this fact? When we speak about living and being in community, what we say and envision is coloured by our different social experiences. Just as our differing cultural contexts influence our attitudes, so do the political systems under which we live. And within the same society, the position from which we speak will make our stories at best complementary but more often disparate and even conflicting.

The voice of those in power is often accepted as the "standard version", while the voices of the small people — those marginalized for various reasons and bearing what the powerful assume to be the stigmas of helplessness, difference and incompetence — go unheard. Is it even possible to grasp the images of community and the visions of unity across differences imposed by injustice? How does the imbalance of power influence our judgments regarding other people?

To speak of our God who shows no partiality is also to reveal our dreams, to tell how we envision what living together will be like when God's purpose for the whole creation is fulfilled. The Bible provides many powerful images of this God-given communion and liberation.

Central themes

• The expression "no longer slave or free" only begins to name the sorts of *divisions in the church between the more powerful and the weaker*. Remember who Paul's converts were: "not many of you were wise by human standards, not many were powerful, not many were of noble birth. But God chose what is foolish in the world to shame the wise; God chose what is weak in the world to shame the strong" (1 Cor. 1:26f.). Early Christianity became well known for its appeal to marginalized peoples, especially for its inclusion of women and slaves.

With an allusion to Genesis 1:27, "male and female God created them", Paul declares that the initial equality of women and men willed by the Creator must now characterize relationships among Christ's people, the new creation. This principle is echoed in Paul's enthusiastic tribute to women colleagues in Romans 16:1-16. The early church struggled with the issue of women's full participation but eventually adopted the patriarchal structures and norms of the societies in which it pursued its mission outreach — just as it adopted other hierarchical structures of the Graeco-Roman world all too easily. Churches today have become more and more clearly aware of the need to take up this struggle once again. We recognize in Galatians 3:28 a constant challenge to reorder relationships in the church and to strive for a fellowship of equals.

How do our societies handle those who seem not to fit the social or economic expectations? How do we deal with the poor, the culturally marginalized, those who have not been part of the long established tradition? Are our failures in this respect as visible as those of the Corinthian congregation, where a few well-off people indulged in sumptuous meals, embarrassing poorer brothers and sisters who were forced to go hungry (1 Cor. 11:21-22)?

In 1998, member churches of the World Council of Churches will account to one another for what they have accomplished during the Ecumenical Decade of Churches in Solidarity with Women (1988-1998). What transformations have occurred in congregations, in synods, in churches? How have churches been instrumental in challenging the standards of behaviour in society? Since the first report on the service and status of women in the churches by the World Council of Churches in 1948, the ecumenical movement has been trying to work for a vision of a Christian community of men and women based on mutual respect and dignity and striving together towards the unity of the church.

• *Unity does not mean sacrificing our diversity*. Rather, it means forgoing the privilege of being a religious insider, of having advantages because of a certain skin colour, of having a particular class status or gender or physical preference. None of these categories should keep us apart or confer any sense of greater importance on some of us than on others. We no longer dare to identify God with our own nation or ethnic group. No longer can we presume male privilege — that God has favoured men in ways denied to women. Never again may we assume any special class status over one another on the basis of economic prosperity or educational advantage. This is the conse-

quence of our being "in Christ". From Soweto to Seattle, from Oslo to Calcutta to Recife, we are all "one in Christ Jesus".

But this picture of unity introduces another problem. In churches made up of one dominant culture or ethnic group, there is a danger of disallowing distinct ethnic identities in the interest of imposing our vision of unity. This seems to have been the consistent experience of those to whom missionaries came in the context of conquest and colonialism during past centuries and in the context of neo-colonialism more recently. But there are other cases in which ethnic or caste affiliation unrelated to outside influences convulses whole nations and is often mirrored in the church. Paul does not seem to envision a unity that is expressed in cultural or even doctrinal uniformity (cf. Rom. 14). Nor did his own missionary outreach attach economic strings to the new congregations which ensured continuing control over them. Rather, members of different groups are called to accept each other's differences. Only by so doing will they liberate each other from impositions and thereby find their own liberation.

The early church aspired to be a new community in which the disenfranchised were accepted as equal participants. However, the economic stratification which existed then continues to be a distressing reality in the churches today. We see it in the greater wealth, power and privilege of denominations in the North, and in the division between rich and poor in congregations everywhere.

The church must constantly bring "strangers" into its fellowship and welcome their distinct spiritual and cultural contributions. As the family of the church grows around the world, we experience our oneness beyond national and even confessional boundaries, and without attaching conditions of race, gender or class to control one another's faith.

Do we see the presence of God in the other? We tend to make things into our own image. So it is with the church: we are inclined to admit people who look like us or at least act like us. The result is that the church becomes our body and not the body of Christ. But the church is not a club for which we can set the rules for membership. As Peter discovered, there is a standard outside of ourselves: all people of faith in Christ Jesus have become part of God's family.

Suggestions for discussion

1. To what extent is your church a hospitable fellowship where all are welcome and valued equally?
2. Who are the marginalized groups in your local community or communities? Do they keep silent or are they attempting to resist? What is your community's response to their resistance or silence?
3. How does your church respond to those marginalized people? Are they present in your congregation or denomination? Are the issues of their cry for survival related to gender? economics? politics? culture? race? Should the church — *your* church — take a role in this struggle?
4. Share some stories of how the passages considered in this study challenge your individual life as well as your life in community.

"Bear One Another's Burdens"

John 13:1-35 — Genesis 18:1-15 — Galatians 6:1-10

Too poor to give. We were very surprised by the reactions of our sisters and brothers from abroad who came to visit our village. Since we had known they were coming, all of us had contributed some money to buy them local handicrafts from the markets. In addition, we agreed that each host family had the liberty to welcome its guests in any way possible.

When we came together afterwards to talk about the visit, we learned that many of the guests had rejected the gifts the families offered. They said they already have enough and we are too poor to give them material things. They will continue to give us mission aid. We can only sing and dance for them.

We now have to ask what justification we have in accepting their money if they cannot accept our small gifts. Is our poverty in big money also to be seen as poverty of hospitality?

The text and context

The story told in John 13:1-35 occurs at a crucial point in the fourth gospel. Jesus has entered Jerusalem and now faces the culmination of his ministry, "his hour" (v.1), the time of his death and glorification. At the opening of his "farewell discourse" (chs 13-17) Jesus calls on his disciples to love one another as he has loved them (cf. vv.1,35). But what does this mean in practice? What do hospitality and love in action look like? Jesus demonstrates this for his disciples in a dramatic and shocking way.

The setting is a meal shared by Jesus and his disciples. At this point in their narratives of Jesus' last days the other gospel writers recount the "words of institution" of the "Last Supper" (Mark 14:17-26; Matt. 26:20-30; Luke 22:14-23), interwoven with the theme of Judas as the one who will betray Jesus. In John 13 the scene is also a meal (vv.2,26-27) and the treachery of Judas is a major theme. But John does not quote the words so familiar to us from our experience of the Lord's supper or eucharist. Instead, he builds his narrative around a surprising act: Jesus washing the feet of his disciples.

The reaction of Peter (vv.6,8) shows that this is not — as one might expect — received gratefully, as a simple act of kindness on Jesus' part. In fact, Peter tries to reject Jesus' act outright. Why should this apparent gesture of courtesy be so offensive, even threatening, to Jesus' disciples?

In Old Testament times foot-washing was an act of courtesy and welcome. It would be offered by a householder to visitors arriving from a journey. After a long trip made in sandals, this act soothed feet that were hot, dusty, sweaty, tired and sore. Abraham offered water to the visitor who brought him news about the son to be born to him and Sarah (Gen. 18:1-15). But if the act was gracious and its purpose noble, the task itself was menial and humbling. It was the proper work of slaves, servants, women and children. Even Abraham seems to have ordered water from some of his servants, for he says, "Let a little water be brought, and wash your feet, and rest yourselves under the tree" (Gen. 18:4). This practice continued through New Testament times.

Like many things we do in communities, including the small things of everyday life, foot-washing established or made visible specific roles and relationships. It reflected the lines of power and subordination within the group. It said clearly, "This person is superior, this person inferior." Yet at the same time it fulfilled a courtesy of hospitality much appreciated by the guest and the host together.

After the foot-washing, Jesus explains to his disciples the significance of this act (vv.12-17). Looking towards his death and resurrection, he gives the disciples a "new commandment": that they "love one another" as he has loved them (v.34). This love should be the distinguishing mark of their community (v.35). It is a love which is realized in mutual humility, hospitality and service to each other.

Central themes

• *Service and life in the Christian community*. In John 13 Jesus the Lord (v.9) washes the feet of his own followers, thus assuming the identity of a slave. In every culture, giving and receiving service belong to familiar patterns of relationship. To break this pattern is unsettling, even frightening. In many cultures to receive service from someone we hold in high esteem is embarrassing; to receive service from someone we consider our equal creates an obligation we may not want to assume; and to accept service from someone we dislike challenges us to give up our antagonisms or old resentments. From our own experience of serving and being served, we can imagine Peter's surprise at Jesus' act, especially when Jesus asked the disciples continually to offer similar service to each other.

Jesus' act is not merely an exceptional display of humility before his disciples, an incident they can forget the next day. Jesus offers this — he commands it — as the pattern of life within the Christian community (vv.13-16): he washes their feet "that you also should do as I have done to you". Perhaps the disciples had come to the supper expecting that Jesus, looking forward to the time when he would no longer be there, would establish clear lines of authority within the community. Instead, he demands of them the same reversal of values as he has displayed in his own ministry, by which the first shall be last, "the Son of Man came not to be served but to serve" (Mark 10:35-45), and "those who want to save their life will lose it" (cf. Mark 8:31-35; 9:33-37; Luke 22:24-27).

We know how easily the language of service can be abused and symbolic actions reduced to isolated practices with no link to wider issues implied. For centuries persons have been kept in menial or degrading roles by defining them in terms of "service" which was in fact servility. Women in particular have been told to accept an inferior status on the ground that "it is their nature to serve others" at the expense of their own identity and dignity. The legacy of the slave trade in the injustice that African Americans still experience is a constant reminder never to take the imagery of service and servant-hood lightly.

This is why Jesus' act is so important — and so threatening. It is no longer those whom we assign to serve who serve. Christ himself, the Master, is the servant. But this is not just a mere reversal of roles.

The disciples must wash *one another's* feet, and such mutual service is to be the organizing principle of their life in community. It is an act of love among equals which is judged by the nature of the relationship rather than the service rendered or gift exchanged.

The service shown by Jesus requires both self-esteem and a deep respect for the person being served. It is rooted in Christian community, just as Jesus was not apart from his disciples but lived and ate and travelled with them. Its effect is to build up not just individuals but also the life of the community as a whole. Those who refuse to give and receive such service exclude themselves from the community (v.8).

Mary anticipates the foot-washing scene by anointing Jesus' feet at her home in Bethany (John 12:1-3). Her act is not a sign of equality; she is criticized for it. Jesus, by doing the same thing, establishes the equality. What causes offence is not just that the leader demonstrates service, but that he insists that his followers do the same, that they wash each other's feet. It is not a service to be expected but a service to be given.

In terms not found in John but used widely elsewhere in the New Testament, koinonia, Christian community, is expressed through diakonia, Christian service. The epistle to the Galatians sees diakonia as mutual helpfulness. It is the hallmark of men and women of faith. Those who do good to others reap the harvest of eternal life (Gal. 6: 1-10).

• *Service and the Lord's supper (eucharist)*. Although John does not explicitly mention the "words of institution" for the Lord's supper (eucharist), sacramental and especially eucharistic themes are prominent in this gospel, and they are developed in ways closely related to the service and self-giving shown in Jesus' act of foot-washing.

These themes are found most fully in chapter 6. The emphasis in John's "eucharistic discourse" (6:25-59) is on how our living relationship with Christ is nurtured through the sharing of his body and blood (vv.51b-58, esp. 57). The eucharist — from a Greek word combining the ideas of "thanksgiving" and "joy" — is a celebration of Christ's presence with his people, a foundation of the idea of *theosis* or our "becoming participants of the divine nature" (2 Pet. 1:4), a repeated sealing of God's new covenant (Mark 14:24; Matt. 26:28; Luke 22:20; 1 Cor. 11:25) and thus a fulfilment of the prophetic hope (Jer. 31:31).

The eucharist is Christ present with his people, but it is Christ the servant, Christ whose body is "broken for you" and whose blood is "poured out for you". The service shown by Jesus in the foot-washing is rooted in this eucharistic vision of Christ's self-giving for all people. It is a vision of unity: it is Christ present with the community, building it up into one body in which all have a place. This is why Paul condemns the wealthy Corinthian believers who were turning the Lord's supper into a private meal, acting as if it belonged to them, satisfying their own needs at the expense of the poor in their midst (1 Cor. 11:17-34). Under such circumstances, says Paul, it is no longer the *Lord's* supper that is being celebrated. The absence of the unity to which the eucharist witnesses is a pain and frustration that lives with the church today. Yet it is that very desire for the unity of the church which gives us hope. We do not hope for what we have, but rather for what we long for and do not have (cf. Rom. 8:24).

Here is also a vision of service beyond the walls of the church. Christ's self-giving for all, celebrated and made present in the eucharist, calls the church to give itself in service to the world. In the eucharist the church offers up the whole creation to God, receiving the gifts of creation each time anew. The eucharist calls for and leads into a "liturgy after the liturgy", a fresh commitment by the community of Christ's followers to work for justice and peace among all humanity and with all of creation. Thus *liturgia* (worship) is linked to *koinonia* (communion) and to *diakonia* (service).

Suggestions for discussion

1. Foot-washing was a common practice in New Testament Palestine but it is rarely practised nowadays. What would be an equivalent personal service in your community and culture which expresses hospitality and humility? Is it practised? Where and when? If not, why not?
2. Consider John 13:1-25 as a call to wider Christian service and action. What do you see as a practice of mutual diakonia equivalent to what Jesus demonstrated by "foot-washing"? Where do you experience it?
3. Take time to think of the relationship of your church with other churches or agencies in which the expression of diakonia involves exchange of money. What important issues does that relationship raise?
4. Think about worship in your own Christian community, especially your celebration of the Lord's supper or eucharist. How does this lead you to service in the world today?
5. Discuss the story at the beginning of this Bible study and think of ways in which the encounter with other cultures or other people contributes to new ways of looking at an issue.

"A Witness Between the Generations"
Joshua 22:10-29 — Deuteronomy 6:20-25 — 2 Timothy 1:1-7

Back to the sources. *During the late 1960s and early 1970s the alienation of young people in many parts of the world from their elders and from the established institutions of society — including the church — became particularly acute. Yet it was precisely at this time that young members of the American Indian community in the USA were beginning to return to their elders and spiritual leaders, eager to regain lost contacts with their religious roots and to deepen their understanding of ancient traditional beliefs and practices. Today American Indian youth are virtually absent from many congregations in denominations founded by missionaries from Europe. What is it in the memories of these hundreds of years of mission history which has caused this retreat?*

A failure to communicate. *"Changing Generations" is a play staged by a youth theatre in Kenya which portrays the struggle of young people who want to maintain community by listening to their parents, but are disappointed that the older generation wants this communication to be a one-way traffic. The youth are expected to listen and the older people to determine what has to be done.*

Two young people who want to marry are unable to obtain consent from either of their families because of a long history of tribal enmity. The young people argue that they do not feel any of this animosity, because they are of a different generation. They have grown up in the city where tribes are not isolated from each other. They have gone to school and church together and played together, and they are unable to share their families' prejudices. Besides, they say, overcoming these old tribal loyalties would be a good thing for the nation and for future generations. But their parents refuse even to hear them. They tell them they are young and naive, rebellious and disobedient, betraying their own family. Worst of all, they are going contrary to the Bible: "Children, obey your parents in the Lord, for this is right" (Eph. 6:1).

The play depicts a total failure of communication. In the end, the young people decide to strike out on their own and begin to make independent decisions, giving up this business of trying to respect "family" and "community".

Text and context

The book of Joshua is understood by Old Testament scholars as part of the historical narrative compiled by the "Deuteronomistic" historian. It incorporates elements of the conquest of the promised land recorded in Deuteronomy into a wider history of the twelve tribes of Israel. The episode described in Joshua 22:10-29 portrays an internal ethnic-religious problem within the newly born united nation, which had just occupied the land of Canaan. It centres on a decision by the tribes of Reuben and Gad and the half-tribe of Manasseh to build an altar apart from the Lord's tabernacle.

The relatively peaceful conquest of the land as portrayed in the book of Joshua was partly due to the role of the groups inhabiting the land before the great immigration of "the Israelites" from Egypt. The text implies (vv.17,20) that the tribes of Reuben and Gad and the half-tribe of Manasseh may have developed a close relationship with local Canaanite groups. This caused a problem for the predominant ethnic group ("the Israelites"), and led them to see the building of an alternative altar as a threat to monotheistic theology. The Israelites gathered at the nation's religious centre (Shiloh), planning to make war against their own marginal (in the sense of being outside the natural geographical boundaries of the land) ethnic groups (v.12). Before launching military action, however, it was agreed to send a fact-finding team, consisting of a priest and the chiefs of tribal families (vv.13,14). They brought the accusation from the Israelites concerning the "treachery" and "rebellion" against the God of Israel and against the unity of the nation (v.19b): "Do not rebel against the Lord, or rebel against *us...*"

The concern of this marginal ethnic group, on the other side, to secure its position within the process of national unity is very important. Anticipating the danger of future isolation, they had made a creative decision: to build a new altar, not for religious ceremonies but as a "witness" between the Israelites and them. In response to their marginal position in the great nation of Israel, they protect themselves from ethnic and religious alienation by employing the most sacred symbol of religious place — an altar — and wisely giving it a new name and a new function: "the altar of Witness". The Hebrew word for "witness", *ed*, used for both the purpose of the altar (vv.27,28) and its name (v.34), may also be an echo of the word *ad* ("pact" or "alliance"), thus suggesting the altar's function as a sign of unity between the tribes. This new altar is not to deny or compete with the ritual function of the central altar in Shiloh — indeed, it is a sign of their loyalty to it — but to protect present and future generations. Their reference to the tabernacle (v.29) is an acknowledgment that there is a single legitimate sanctuary of the tribal federation, thought to have been at Shiloh.

The older generation plays a significant role in this process of reconciliation. The chiefs of all the Israelite tribes (vv.13-14) belonged to the generation of the "later wilderness period", who had witnessed the struggle of the Israelites in the desert with God and nature. Without their approval, civil war would have been inevitable. This witnessing function is confirmed in Deuteronomy 6:20-25, where the older generation is called upon to remind younger generations of the "great and awesome signs and wonders" by which the Lord brought about the salvation of Israel from bondage to the superpower Egypt.

This model of handing down the message of God's salvation in the context of the nation as a family is preserved in New Testament times. In 2 Timothy 1:5 it is noteworthy that "faith" is said to have been handed down from the grandmother Lois to her daughter Eunice and then to Timothy as a church leader. But while Paul commends this intergenerational passing down of faith, his choice of the young Timothy as his successor speaks even a greater message. Paul appreciated the fact that Timothy, young as he was, had stayed with him when every one of his companions in Asia had turned away from him (2 Tim. 1:15). The letters to Timothy relate Paul's deep reliance on his faithful friendship, and he admonishes the young man to remain firm in his faith and not to let anyone "despise" his youth (1 Tim. 4:12).

The lesson of the Timothy story seems to be that, while the older generations have a responsibility to pass on faith, the young people must be given space to live out that faith. To tell about faith is a good thing; to live out that faith is the most desirable thing to do. Timothy as a leader had to take full responsibility for what he needed to do. His grandmother, mother and Paul could give him clues and share their experiences, but Timothy himself had to sort out all the advice given to him and construct a way to be a young church leader.

Central themes

• *Tradition*. This word is often understood as referring to a fixed set of beliefs that defines the identity of one's own sector of the Christian community. When "tradition" in this sense is used to imply that there can be no change in how the faith is understood, expressed or lived out, it can be an obstacle to church unity and a barrier to listening to prophetic new voices. But the word itself has a much more dynamic meaning, for "tradition" refers not only to the deposit of truth but also to the process of handing it down from generation to generation in a continuing dialogue which keeps it fresh and relevant in each new situation. This dynamic understanding is echoed in the reference to Timothy's "sincere faith... that *lived* first in your grandmother Lois and your mother Eunice and now... *lives* in you" (2 Tim. 1:5). Keeping the tradition alive within the Christian community is a matter of continuing commitment ("rekindle the gift of God that is within you", v.6), lived out within the structured fellowship of the community ("through the laying on of my hands", v.6) and ensured by the power of God (compare v.14: "guard the good treasure... with the help of the Holy Spirit living in us").

• *Witness to the generations*. The tribes that built the altar on the Jordan were concerned to transmit the faith within their own families across the years. The altar was to be a witness to faith and faithfulness not only for the moment but also for "your children" and "our children" (vv.25,27). An important task of parents in the history of Israel was to inculcate in their children the meaning of the faith by teaching them about the people's deliverance from slavery (Deut. 6:20-25). Recognizing this role of the family can help to correct a one-sided individualism which places all the emphasis on a personal decision. Families can pass on faith — sometimes in words, some-

times in praying or worshipping together, sometimes simply in the way they live together. But the very elements of closeness and shared experience which can make families a privileged place of dialogue between generations can sometimes turn oppressive and prevent people from being open to the grace of God or life in committed community.

• *Memory and memories.* What Reuben, Gad and the half tribe of Manasseh built along the Jordan was a "copy of the altar", meant to keep alive in the memory of future generations that all twelve tribes belonged together and were committed to staying together. Shared memories can be a powerful force for holding people together. But memory is neither an infallible guide to understanding the past nor a guarantee of preserving community. Selective memory may allow us to overlook the past injustices committed by our own community and even to justify maintaining oppression of others. Partial memories of past conflicts may breed resentments and animosities that feed hatred and fear, so that we refuse even to consider the possibility of costly reconciliation to break the cycle of division and conflict.

Suggestions for discussion

1. "When you look at your toothless grandmother, count your own teeth." This African proverb is a reminder that the older generation of today were yesterday's youth. It is used to instil respect for older people in the community. What are your community's concerns in regard to ageing?
2. Look around your own congregation. What part do people under 30 play on management committees of the church, in worship, in prayer meetings and Bible study groups?
3. What programmes in your community are designed to help to create understanding of the needs and concerns of young people? Are there any joint events besides worship in which youth and "elders" meet regularly for talking or working together?
4. How does your church deal with reports and recommendations from local and international youth gatherings?
5. Look at the stories at the beginning of this study. What do they say to you? What stories would you tell in your context to illustrate how the tradition of faith is communicated in history and the constraints that arise with new times and new people?

"A Cloud of Witnesses"

Hebrews 11:1-3, 11:39-12:2

Living in hope. Hope! Whenever I hear that word, my heart starts pounding in my breast and it feels like it will swell up like a balloon. But I'm abnormal, so I cannot join normal people. Most deaf people are frustrated in the face of hope and are leading desperate lives with bitter hearts. I want to shout, "Deaf people too should live in hope!" This may be talking to myself. I don't know. People who lost hope are like people who have lost their souls. I will live with hope even though I can feel my hope perishing like water bubbles (from Eun Seong Son, aged 14, in *What It Is Like To Be Me*, ed. Helen Exley, New York, Friendship Press, 1984, p.44).

Our heroes of faith. During an international conference, participants were asked to think of people — past or present, dead or living, real or mythical, canonized by the church or largely unknown — whom they perceived as witnesses of faith. Their names were to be written on large sheets of paper pasted to the wall. By the last day, the wall was covered with names, some written in full, others only initials. It was a moving sight. Some were world-famous; others national and local people. They included St Paul, Mary the mother of Jesus, Nelson Mandela, Calvin, Helen Keller, Abraham, Moses, JFK, the Hebrew midwives, Martin Luther King, the Pope, Auntie B, Archbishop Tutu, Mother Teresa, Helder Camara, Esther, the Women in Black, Ruth, HJ, feminist theologians, Rahab, my mother, the missionary who paid my school fees, Rebecca, the policeman who testified for me in a rape case, Accama the Dalit woman, the pastor who stood in solidarity with me when I "came out", the mothers of the Plaza de Mayo, the murdered nuns, the UN soldiers risking their lives on the war fronts, Fr Fernando, my grandmother…

*With no order or hierarchy given to the list, with the writing done
in various colours of pens, with the legibility varying from clear to
near-hieroglyphics, the picture that emerged could have had no other
title but "a cloud of witnesses".*

Text and context

Chapters 11 and 12 of the letter to the Hebrews are widely
known as the chapters on faith. Chapter 11 has even been called the
"Faith Hall of Fame". Beginning with a brief "definition" — "Now
faith is the assurance of things hoped for, the conviction of things
not seen" (11:1) — the author launches into a detailed description
of faith, complete with references to several dozens of models of
faith.

From the beginning of this passage, words like "assurance" and
"conviction" lay the foundation for the close link between faith and
hope. Hope is an expectation linked to faith, and faith is not merely an
intellectual frame of mind. Faith involves action. Hope is marked by
the assurance that what God promises will indeed come true (10:39).
Hope is the conviction that the death and resurrection of Jesus Christ,
upon which the past and the present are assured, is indeed a fact and
not an illusion.

The heroes of faith listed in 11:4-38 are people who acted out their
faith as they lived their hope in God. Abraham is affirmed for obeying
God and migrating to Canaan (Gen. 12:1-4) and for his confidence
that his descendants would possess the land in which he himself would
only be a sojourner (Gen. 15:16-18).

Careful readers will encounter a few discrepancies when they
compare this chapter with the parallel passages in the Old Testament.
For example, the Old Testament does not say that the motive for
Abel's sacrifice was faith (compare v.4 with Gen. 4:1-5). The
reference to Sarah in relation to Abraham (v.11) is ambiguous in the
original text, leading to a great deal of discussion among translators,
as will be evident from a comparison of different versions. Some
believe that the text attributes faith to Sarah: because she believed in
God's faithfulness she received the power to conceive a child. Others
consider the grammatical form of the sentence as attributing faith to
Abraham, while Sarah is only associated with him. Many instances of
faith connected to Moses (vv.23-28) differ from the parallel passages

in the Old Testament, as comparing the texts will show and consulting good commentaries can help to explain.

The first action of faith associated with Moses is the faith of his parents for defying the pharaoh's order. Not listed in Hebrews are the women who supported this plot. One set of witnesses to faith are the two midwives, Shiphrah and Puah (Ex. 1:15-22), who did not kill the baby boys born to Hebrew women, Moses' mother Jochebed and his sister Miriam. But the pharaoh's daughter and her maids were also accomplices in the plot (Ex. 2:1-10). It does not seem possible that the daughter of the pharaoh could be ignorant that the baby Moses was a Hebrew boy who was accordingly expected to die by her father's decree. These actions of civil disobedience and solidarity among women signify hope, which is active resistance against adversity, destruction, evil and the void of hopelessness. Hope refuses to accept defeat, because those who hope put their trust in God, who is the foundation of hope. Hope entails risk. Like faith, it depends entirely on God.

In Hebrews 11:32-38 the author begins another long list of Old Testament heroes of faith, only some of whom are then named since, as the author observes, time and space do not allow mention of all the witnesses of faith. The grand finale (12:1ff.) is that, since we are surrounded by such a cloud of witnesses, there is no reason to lose hope. Hope is to be lived. Hope like faith involves action. Faith resembles a difficult race, in which the eyes of the runner are fixed on the prize to be won. Jesus, who endured great suffering for our sakes (12:2-3), is held up as the ultimate goal for hope.

Faith as portrayed in this epistle is not cheap or sugar-coated. Many of these heroes of faith did not receive the promise they hoped for. Some ended up flogged and destitute (11:36-38). Some died horrible deaths. There is no guarantee of luxury or an easy life given to those who have faith in God and hope for God's reign. It can be difficult and disappointing. Yet faith calls for a constant commitment to believe God no matter what. From a faith perspective, this means claiming accountability from the one who holds out the promise of hope, the one whom we hold accountable for making good our hopes. While acknowledging the realism of disappointment, frustration, anger, brokenness and even despair, to have faith and hope means to engage with life hour by hour in such a way that our actions express what we hope for. To hope for justice and peace means to work for the elimination of injustice and to be a peacemaker. To hope for democracy means to practise being democratic in our relationships, beginning with those closest to us. To hope for wholeness means to face our brokenness with courage and be willing to change.

Bishop Don Helder Camara must have understood this when he said: "We must have no illusions. We must not be naive. If we listen to the voice of God, we make our choice, get out of ourselves and fight nonviolently for a better world. We must not expect to find it easy; we shall not walk on roses; people will not throng to hear us and applaud; and we shall not always be aware of divine protection. If we are to be pilgrims of justice and peace, we must expect the desert."

Central themes

• *Faith* is a key term in Christian theology. Hebrews 11:1 is phrased in the form of a definition of faith, but in reality it is an explanation of how faith is lived. In the Bible, to have faith is to "have faith in" and is synonymous with "believing". To say that Abraham had faith in God (Gen. 15:6) means that he put his trust in God, he believed God. "To trust", "to believe" and "to have faith in" form a family of words often used interchangeably.

• *Witness* is a juridical term. The Old Testament prohibits false and malicious witness (Ex. 20:16; 23:1-3; Deut. 19:15-19). In the New Testament, the witness theme is central to the gospel of John, the Acts of the Apostles, the letter to the Hebrews and the Revelation. In the epistle to the Hebrews, the focus is on the faith of the witnesses. The list of people in the Hebrews is sometimes associated with saints.

Suggestions for discussion

1. Who have been models of courage for you because of the way they have lived out the Christian gospel? What is it that has challenged you in their life and actions?
2. Can you think of a time when saying Yes to God means or might mean saying No to some presently accepted value or system?
3. Faith and hope are words which are often talked about together. What do you hope for?

4. Especially in churches that follow a liturgical calendar and a lectionary, this text from the epistle to the Hebrews is often used as one of the readings in connection with the commemoration of the saints. The subject of saints is an especially interesting one for discussion in ecumenical groups, not only because different traditions honour different saints (and the saints of one tradition may be the heretics of another!), but also because of the differences in how they understand the role of saints.

5. The theme of the WCC's eighth assembly is "Turn to God — Rejoice in Hope". Talk about these words. Which biblical passages speak to this theme in your context? What is your joy — what are you celebrating?

PART II

Meditations

Introductory Note

Each of these six meditations focusses on an aspect of the assembly theme "Turn to God — Rejoice in Hope".

Weaving together biblical passages, stories and personal accounts, and commentary, the meditations are suitable for a wide range of uses. They may be the starting-point for personal reflection based on the biblical texts referred to and the testimonies from Christians in many different situations who are seeking to live out their faith today. Pastors will find the material useful in a variety of ways: as the basis for a cycle of prayer or meditation in their congregations; as background material for congregational or ecumenical discussion groups; as material — to be used as is or in adapted form — for church newsletters or magazines; or as starter texts for sermons.

These meditations were developed from material provided by Christians from all around the world, representing many different confessions and life-situations. May the Spirit strengthen all those who, using this material, seek to *turn to God*, and empower them truly to *rejoice in hope*.

Turning to the Living God

"Come, let us return to the Lord" (Hosea 6:1) is, as the prophet himself points out, one of the easiest things to say and one of the hardest things to work out in our lives. In a later chapter (11:1-11), we are given a picture of what such turning to God means. We are like rebellious children, learning to walk. Our parent is always standing by with open arms ready to put us on our feet again when we fall, but we still stumble on until calamity occurs. Then we cry out in despair and finally turn to the one who has been waiting all along to help us. We are able then to make a new start, relying on strength other than our own. But it also requires a new determination to get it right this time.

For Mary Smith, one of the homeless women living at an emergency shelter in Washington D.C., turning to God meant taking steps towards recovery from addiction to drugs and alcohol, facing broken relationships, beginning treatment for physical illness and opening herself to the community of caring people around her. The result has been a new life for her — one that has required much courage and faith, but that is now full of happiness and hope.

Such turning involves new relationships. A whole community of "turning ones" are called to share the good news of a God who accepts all who turn, even those who might fear rejection. Lawrence, an African American theological student, was dying of AIDS. Yet he persisted in trying to complete his seminary course. When it was clear that his time would run out before he could complete the course, the seminary organized a private ceremony in the chapel to award him an honorary degree, honouring one whom God had honoured in a covenant of constant love.

This covenant of love was embodied in the coming of Jesus into the world. To prepare to receive him, John the Baptist called on the people to turn to God in repentance, *metanoia* — a Greek word whose literal meaning is change of mind. John explained in practical terms what the effects of such *metanoia* would be: generosity, fair dealings, no bullying (Luke 3:10-14). Jesus echoed that call to repentance as he announced the breaking in of the kingdom of God within the life of the world (Mark 1:15). "Repent, and believe in the good news" was his invitation. The kingdom of God could be experienced here and now in the lives of those who turned towards it in faith. For the first disciples, "turning" to the one who announced such good news meant walking all the way with Christ, learning to embrace and live out the values of God's kingdom. That way led finally to the cross, and beyond that to the resurrection and then to the commission to go out into all the world and proclaim the gospel to all people, baptizing them and teaching them to observe all that Jesus had taught (Matt. 28:19,20).

At a conference held in Rustenburg, South Africa, in 1991, leaders of the white Dutch Reformed Church confessed that they had "changed their minds" about apartheid. They had been wrong in believing it to be in accordance with the will of God, and now they repented of that. A black African Christian was heard to comment quietly, "I shall believe in their repentance when they show that they have changed not only their minds but also their way of life!"

So the call to turn to God is a call to repentance, to a change of mind and of heart, both on the part of individuals and of nations. Many nations today are guilty of injustice, genocide, corruption, greed and oppression of the poor; and all need to repent and turn back to the God who requires justice, mercy and humility (Micah 6:6-8). In many parts of the world, such a prophetic call is costly, and there have been many Christian martyrs in this century who, like the prophets of old, have cried out in God's name for justice for the oppressed and liberation for the captives. On the tomb of Bishop Muge of Kenya, champion of the poor, who was killed in a road accident while out on a pastoral visit to displaced peoples, the words of Amos 5:24 are engraved: "Let justice flow on like a river and righteousness like a never failing torrent."

The strength to make such a witness even in the face of death comes from the confidence of those who, having turned to God, know that their own sins have been forgiven (Psalm 51) and that they now share in a new humanity, living in the power of resurrection life

(Rom. 6:1-14). Some people say, "You can't change human nature."
But human nature *can* be changed once it is given back into the hands
of the God who created it and can make it new. It should be as natural
for people to turn to God as it is for a bird to migrate to its new resting
place (Jer. 8:4ff.). For God has made a new covenant with human
beings and will, if they repent, write a new law in their hearts (Jer.
31:31).

God is always seeking us, drawing us back to turn again to the one
who keeps the covenant of love with us. That covenant has been
expressed most visibly in the broken body of Christ and has been
sealed in his blood. So every eucharist is another turning to accept that
love for ourselves and for one another. It requires us to submit our
lives to God and to resolve to be and act only according to God's will.
To turn to the living God means that we join ourselves to the
community of all who are penitent, to be one in Christ — one Body of
Christ — working out together what his love means for the life of the
world.

The God to Whom We Turn

"In the beginning God..." The opening words of the Bible affirm that everything begins in God and belongs to God, the Creator and Sustainer of the universe. The design was good (Gen. 1:31). Even though it is evident that now all is not well with this world, the Creator has made a bond with all living things, promising to preserve them from final destruction (Gen. 9:15f.). That covenant was particularly applied to a people through whom God promised to bless all nations of the earth (Gen. 12:1-3). It was a twofold covenant. The God who promised to keep faith with the people demanded that in return the people should keep faith with God. The terms of the covenant were spelled out for the people in the book of the law. They had the choice. They could either walk in the way of God, who would accompany them throughout their whole journey, or they could go their own way, a way which would lead to destruction (Deut. 30:16-21). The covenant was sealed in blood, as many ancient treaties were (Ex. 24:7f.).

Despite the fact that human beings have not kept their side of the covenant, God has constantly renewed the promises for all who would turn back from their own way to seek God's forgiveness. God's love for us is like a womb in which we are nurtured, surrounded by what the Hebrew scriptures call "loving-kindness", *chesed*, the feeling of a mother for the child she carries within her. That love is there long before we are aware of it, and it pursues us even when we turn away from it (Psalm 51). It is a love which forms a bond with us that lasts throughout our lives, yet it sets us free to find our own feet and walk in our own way.

This human freedom can lead us astray into new captivities. We become prisoners to our own selfishness, or we become victims of the greed and oppression of others. But still that love of God follows us, longing to set us free from all that would prevent us from growing into our full stature as the children of God. As God said to Moses, "I have observed the misery of my people... I have heard their cry... and I have come down to deliver them" (Ex. 3:7). Those who turn to such a God find that their own ears also become attuned to the cry of the oppressed and they are drawn into God's liberating purpose.

The pharaohs of today's world exercise many kinds of power, and the misery of the people takes terrible forms — hunger, poverty, war, torture and imprisonment, rape and violence against women. In some places such violations of human rights are even given religious and legal sanction. Yet in the midst of this mess those who turn to God, the Creator and Sustainer of all humanity, find that help is near. In Pakistan the tiny Christian community experienced this recently when the life of a young Christian boy was threatened. He had been falsely accused of making derogatory remarks about the prophet Muhammad. Along with two Christian men he was thrown into jail and sentenced to death. The Christian community prayed and fasted on their behalf and called on Christians throughout the world to join them in intercession. Eminent Muslim lawyers came to the prisoners' aid, and finally they were found not guilty and were released. The Christian community rejoiced with them that God's promise had been fulfilled. They sang a psalm which expresses God's promise:

> Those who love me, I will deliver;
> I will protect those who know my name.
> When they call to me, I will answer them;
> I will be with them in trouble,
> I will rescue them and honour them (Psalm 91:14f.).

Such promises sustain God's people in all times of suffering and keep alive the hope of liberation. Throughout the long years of struggle for freedom in Namibia, the church kept reminding the people that they were made in the image of God, who would keep faith with them and free them from their bondage. They trusted in God's faithfulness even though at times, amid all the killing and the hatred, it seemed as if God were no longer with them. When the day of freedom came, the church called on the people to turn to God again through both repentance and service. For the churches, that meant preparing for the return of the refugees and helping to repatriate them. When unemployment among those returning created a crisis in the country, the Council of Churches in Namibia negotiated with the government to find them work. Turning to God means seeking to heal the wounds inflicted by war, working for reconciliation between those who were once enemies and welcoming home again those who have been far away.

Jesus compared returning to God to a homecoming. The well-known story of the prodigal son (Luke 15:11-32) gives a most vivid picture of the God to whom we turn. The son who had broken away from home turned back again only when he was in desperate need. Then he "came to himself" (v.17). The Aramaic original behind the Greek word translated this way is the equivalent of "repented", meaning that he realized the enormity of his offence and was full of remorse. Considering himself no longer worthy to be treated as a son, he begs simply to be treated as a servant. But the father takes the initiative and welcomes him with such accepting love that the sinner can do no other than respond. There is no more mention of being anything but a son. Even his more righteous brother has to learn how to welcome the penitent and share the father's joy at his homecoming. Such is the love of the God to whom we turn, who bids us to accept one another as we ourselves are accepted and loved.

Marks of a Life Turned to God

"Who do you say that I am?", Jesus asked his disciples (Mark 8:29). This was a long time after they had first turned to him. They had been with him on many journeys through the towns and villages of Galilee. They had seen many signs, they had learned many lessons, they had listened to many words. But now comes the crucial question. Jesus asks them pointedly to declare their allegiance. Peter almost stumbles on the truth. "You are the Messiah." That marks the turning-point, not only in Peter's understanding, but in the gospel story itself. Jesus begins his journey towards Jerusalem and spells out for his disciples the cost of a life turned wholly towards God. It will be marked by the sign of the cross (Mark 8:34).

Many Christians experience that kind of turning-point in their lives. Their Christian faith cannot be described solely in terms of belief or practice but becomes a total commitment, taking their lives in a new direction in obedience to the call of Christ. It is a costly discipleship, demanding the renunciation of everything that would hold us back, whether self-interest, worldly ambition, even family ties. Nothing must be allowed to take priority over our relationship to Christ. With Jesus there can be no halfway measures.

A team of evangelists visiting a village in Togo was challenged by one of the local people: "I have the impression that several of your Christian friends have conflicting feelings. They still believe in the protection of our local god and call on him on certain important occasions in their lives, while claiming all the while to follow your God. Are not such people half pagan, half Christian?" This is a question that could be put to Christians anywhere who still cling to "gods" of their own, whether the materialistic idols of the modern world or more ancient superstitions. We need to name those idols to which so many people in the modern world are enslaved: money, ambition, power, drugs, sex, violence.

Two stories from prisons in different parts of the world show how lives that have once been marked, even marred, by addiction to such idols can turn to the cross and receive instead the mark of compassion and commitment. A prisoner who for five years had been part of a Methodist prayer group meeting in the cell-blocks had tried hard to free himself from addiction to drugs. But they had taken a firm hold on him. Each time he was released from prison his old mates caught up with him and drew him back into his bad habits. Finally the drug addiction destroyed him. In his last days he turned back to God, seeing Christ dying for him on the cross. His one concern then was that his children and their friends should be saved from exposure to the dangers that had destroyed his own life. He died as one who had made his own peace with God and who took with him to the grave the promise of his pastor that he and the whole Christian community would commit themselves to befriending the younger generation and doing all they could to combat the vices that threatened their lives.

Such a commitment demands of those who make it more than just concern or charity. Compassion literally means "suffering with" those who suffer. A pastor tells the story of a manager who was confronted in his office by an ex-convict who came in desperate need of help to start a new life. The man had been in jail for 23 years after committing violent murder. He still had a knife in his belt. Prompted at first by an instinct of self-preservation, the manager was inclined just to give the man some money and send him away. But some words he had heard in a sermon only the Sunday before thundered through his head. "Ministry", the preacher had said, "is self-forgetfulness in the fertile fields of love." The ex-convict needed more than money. He needed someone who would dare to risk loving him. The manager decided to take that risk and to give his visitor not just his money but his time, promising to do all he could to help him. One of the marks of turning to God is taking the risks of love.

Such love is always costly. One Good Friday the members of a congregation in an inner city church in London were singing Passiontide hymns in the forecourt of their church as an act of witness to the local community. They were joined briefly by a young West Indian who was working in a McDonald's restaurant across the street. When he went back into the restaurant a fight ensued, and the young man was stabbed by two white youths. He staggered back to the church and died there on the steps as the congregation were singing:

See from his head, his hands, his feet
Sorrow and love flow mingled down;
Did e'er such love and sorrow meet
Or thorns compose so rich a crown?

Some months later a visitor came to the church from many miles away. Introducing herself as the mother of the young man who had been murdered, she said she had come both to meet the women who had nursed him in his dying moments and to visit the youths who had stabbed him, and who were now in prison. "I know that God loved this world so much that he gave his only Son for the sake of sinners," she said, "and I loved my son so much that I too must love even those who sinned against him."

Forgiveness, compassion, commitment — these are the marks of those who, having turned to God themselves through the cross of Jesus, find the strength to love.

Turning to a Living Hope

"May God, who is the ground of hope, fill you with all joy and peace as you lead the life of faith until, by the power of the Holy Spirit, you overflow with hope" (Rom. 15:13). The Bible is a book overflowing with hope.

Hebrew has many different words to describe hope. One of them is related to the word for a rope, suggesting the support a mountaineer clings to even when the distant summit is still far away and wreathed in clouds. Another word suggests a place of refuge where one can shelter from the storm and not be buffeted by it. Another word suggests waiting and the patience it often requires. Hope is both a noun and a verb. It is a virtue which rests on the promises of God, and it is an action which energizes those who turn to God. "Steadfast love surrounds those who trust in the Lord," says the psalmist (Psalm 32:10).

Christian hope is a miracle because it transcends the normal laws of cause and effect. The reality of our sinful world is such that we might well find the future frightening. Yet hope refuses to accept defeat. In even the most difficult situations Christians hold on to the hope that what is bad will pass and that what is good will be preserved.

"When the catastrophe arrives," said St John Chrysostom, "do not fall into despair, and real hope will help you to stand firm amidst danger... Do not despair, and do not fall spiritually if you do not receive what you expected quickly."

So Christians strive to live in such a way that their deeds express what they hope for. To hope for justice means to work for justice; to hope for peace means to become a peacemaker. Hope, faith and love stand together above all human reasoning and the laws by which the world is ruled. This trinity of virtues form the foundation of the truly Christian life.

"Hope is faith in one's work, the door of love; hope destroys despair and is the pledge of our future welfare," wrote Holy John Leslvenshchich.

The Orthodox catechism speaks often about hope. It is hope which gives quietness of heart, as we trust in God to look after our salvation and to bestow on us the promised blessedness. If we conscientiously examine our own lives, we are all bound to admit that, measured against the teaching of the gospel, we deserve condemnation, not eternal blessedness. Yet in spite of everything, we can put our trust and hope in a merciful God who will lead us to eternal life. Without this living hope spiritual life becomes impossible. Despair, defined in the teaching of the ascetics as the lack of living hope, is a mortal sin, the opposite of the life God intends us to enjoy.

"The unreasonable human attitude is sinning in both cases, hoping to extend our physical life by enjoying the pleasures of this world to the detriment of spiritual hope. The soul becomes alien to real hope, leaning on uncertainties and not mastering them, and hope does not receive what it is waiting for," wrote St Gregory of Palamas.

"Hope without patience cannot exist," wrote Father Tihon Zadonski in his *Teaching on Salvation*. "Where there is real hope there is patience and where there is patience there is hope, which is exposed to many temptations. We are tempted when losing worldly goods, when losing health, honour or our standard of living, to fall into many afflictions. In such a disastrous situation it is essential not to look for doubtful ways of avoiding it but to surrender to God's will and to wait for God's mercy in helping us to be patient and to be delivered from evil."

Those who turn to God in hope can begin living in the present as though the future were already here. Even in our divided world, we can begin to anticipate that unity to which God is calling us.

One sign of such hope is to be seen wherever Christians of different denominations come together to worship and to work together for a world of harmony.

In Milton Keynes, a new city in England, the Church of Christ the Cornerstone is home to congregations of Anglicans, Baptists, Methodists, Roman Catholics and United Reformed churches who have signed a covenant, pledging to come together as closely as they can and to grow together. Their five-denominational ecumenical church building stands like a cathedral of hope, where all share in a varied weekday pattern of prayer, Bible study and service.

There are still many hopes to be realized. Christians in Milton Keynes long for the day when all five traditions will be able to share full communion, and when racial tensions within the city as a whole will have been resolved. Yet many aspects of shared life which seemed unthinkable only a few years ago have now become a reality. They are able to live and work as a shared community, sharing their lives with people of differing abilities, and helping many who are in need through a City Counselling Centre.

Such an ecumenical community is a foretaste of what is yet to come. No one knows where God will lead the church next, any more than we know what the future of the ecumenical movement will be. But we are called to travel on in the faith that God will give us the courage to dream dreams, to plant seeds of hope and thus to catch a glimpse of the glory yet to be revealed.

Rejoicing in Hope

God has given us "a new birth into a living hope through the resurrection of Jesus Christ from the dead", declares the writer of the First Letter of Peter. This is reason for "an indescribable and glorious joy" (1 Pet. 1:3,8).

On the face of it, the people to whom this letter was addressed had little to rejoice about. They are referred to as "exiles of the Dispersion" (1:1), and the many allusions in the letter to the reality of suffering suggest that they were people who met with hostility in the communities where they were regarded as aliens. Some students of the New Testament believe that this letter was part of a homily preached at services of baptism. It emphasizes strongly that those who are baptized into Christ share both in his death and in the hope of his resurrection. Baptism is like dying to self and being born into a whole new way of living, with a joy that no power on earth can destroy.

Birth always is a sign of hope. At a time of great national distress, the prophet Isaiah reassured King Ahaz that a child would be born who would bring new hope of peace (Isa. 9:6). During the darkest times of the second world war, when the Czech people were occupied by hostile forces, a baby was born to a Christian couple. They named her Nadeje, which means "Hope". Throughout the years when she was growing up the prospect for the Czech people seemed bleak. But always Nadeje's parents clung to their faith that nothing the powers of this earth might do could take away the hope given to the world by the resurrection of Jesus. "Because I live, you shall live also" were words of faith which they passed on to their daughter. This living hope still inspires her, particularly when she is able to gather with two or three others in the name of Christ and senses the risen presence of Christ as they share together the Lord's supper.

It was such a hope that inspired John Hus (1372-1415), the great Czech reformer, who was prepared even to die for Christ's sake. That same hope can inspire the Czech people today to share with their neighbours, even those who are without God and without hope in this world, the good news that they too can be born again into a living hope through the resurrection of Christ. Like the Christians of the early church to whom the First Letter of Peter was addressed, they are learning what it means to be ready to give an accounting for the hope that is in them, always doing so with courtesy and respect (1 Pet. 3:15).

It has been said that every new baby is a sign of God's continuing faith in humanity. In England, on a day when the newspapers were full of threats about the growing numbers of immigrants coming into the country and statistics were being tossed about in an attempt to alarm people about population growth, a West Indian mother in a London hospital gave birth to a beloved daughter. Like those Czech parents she too called her daughter Hope, and the members of the congregation where that baby was baptized committed themselves to trying to build a community where every child of every race is truly welcomed as a child of God. Baptism marks that birth into a new community where we enter into unity with one another as we all share in the life of the risen Lord.

It sometimes seems as though we must live today as a community of hope in a culture of hopelessness. A minister from Australia writes of a visit he once paid to Smokey Mountain in Metro Manila, a shanty town built on a massive garbage dump. In this wasteland, amidst the smells and pollution, a whole community has taken shape. People have built their own homes out of waste products; they busy themselves collecting saleable bits and pieces of garbage in order to raise cash. The children in their tattered clothes grin cheekily. Down in the mud among the broken plant pots, the visitor caught a glimpse of a bright red geranium blooming. It seemed to breathe life, to symbolize hope in the midst of apparent hopelessness, joy in the midst of chaos and suffering. The resurrection of Jesus the Christ comes to us like that bright red flower. But unlike any earthly flower, it is a living hope, genuine and eternal, that will never fade.

That sense of Christ's living presence can speak its word of hope to people of all cultures. A young Thai woman who spent some time studying in the United States felt totally alienated in a strange land.

Often alone, having made few friends, she would seek solace and quietness by entering a church. Though she had had no instruction in the Christian faith, the stillness and beauty of the building, the pictures and the candles, the chiming of the bells and the gathering of the people around the altar all spoke to her of a living presence to whom she wanted to draw near. When she arrived back home in Thailand, she sought out a Christian pastor and said, "I really feel God wants me to become a Christian." The pastor assured her that her search was the result of God's own initiative in seeking her. After instruction in the Christian faith she was baptized and entered into all the joy of a worshipping and witnessing community.

But as for the early Christians, witness in our century may also mean martyrdom. Indeed, the church of the 20th century has known more martyrs than at any other time in Christian history. Among them were the Christians in Germany during the Nazi period who realized that Christianity and National Socialism were incompatible. Both demand total allegiance. Among those confessing the Christian faith was Count Helmuth von Moltke, whose story has recently been made into a television film based on his letters and speeches. At his trial for his so-called "treason" in opposing Nazism, he affirmed confidently that though Hitler had prophesied that his Reich would last a thousand years, Christians believe that the only eternal kingdom is the kingdom of Christ. In the strength of that faith, and fortified by a final eucharist celebrated in prison with his wife and pastor, Helmuth von Moltke walked fearlessly to face his executioners, rejoicing in the hope that has shone round the martyrs throughout all the centuries of the church's life.

The Hope of the Nations

"I saw a new heaven and a new earth" (Rev. 21:1). The description which follows that vision is detailed enough for a city-planner's drawing board. The city the seer describes has twelve open gates, walls studded with jewels, fruit trees decked in health-giving leaves and a stream of clear water running through the city centre. It is a cosmopolitan city where people of all nations are at home. It never closes its doors, and there are no security risks. It needs no temple, for all are aware of God's presence in their midst. It is a city of our dreams.

How different it is from the cities most of us inhabit! This decade began with a symbol of hope, the dismantling of the Berlin Wall. It seemed then like answered prayer and hope fulfilled. Yet that breaking of the barrier between Eastern and Western Europe, between socialism and capitalism, seems now to have opened the way for communal wars and for personal insecurity in the hearts of many Europeans. For many, what looked like a new beginning has seemed to mark the end of hope. The ruins of Sarajevo stand as a grim reminder of the temptation in our times to deny the cosmopolitan vision and let national and confessional animosities from the past continue to define our attitudes to one another today. Across the world, all our cities are being challenged to find ways of welcoming the stranger, of living together with peoples of diverse cultures, of creating a healthy environment, of showing the reverence for one another which comes from awareness of God's presence among us all.

For we are not only what history has made us to be. Our identity as Christians is defined not by what we are, but by what we could be. To live in hope is to live with an open future and to be inspired by the possibility of change. God has given us a glimpse of the "secret plan", a plan for the fullness of time, when all things, the whole universe, literally the *oikoumene* will be gathered up together to live in the unity which Christ will give (Eph. 1:10). We as Christians are called to live as though that vision for the end of all time shapes our life-style today. We have the firm promise of God on which to build our hope.

Suppose that we had no such vision or promise. Suppose that an angel of God were to announce that there is no hope of a new heaven and a new earth, that there are no streets of gold, no tree with healing leaves, for God has withdrawn the promises. No longer then could we turn to God and rejoice in hope. Our churches would feel like giving up. Our ecumenical programmes would seem to be doomed.

Looking only at the scenario of today's world, hope may seem very distant. Some may even believe that the world as we know it is coming to an end. The end of a millennium inevitably provokes prophets of doom. Yet to those who look for signs of God's secret plan already revealing itself, the very place where hope is to be found is in the midst of brokenness. It is in times of greatest despair in a nation's history that the vision shines most clearly. This is how it was in South Africa during the darkest days of oppression and repression. It was during those days that the *Kairos Document* was written, that the "Standing for Truth" campaign gained momentum, that young people challenged the oppressors' guns, that the clergy marched on the parliament buildings. These were visionary actions, driven by hope.

There is an old tradition in African communities who lived in dry places where the only source of water was the river. When the river became polluted by human beings and animals, the people devised a way of overcoming the problem of pollution by digging down deep on the side of the river. Fresh, clean water would gush out. Likewise, in the seemingly hopeless situation that existed in South Africa right until the beginning of this decade, Christians and all communities of faith had to "dig deep" to find the hope that would give them the strength to act. They had to give "an accounting for the hope" that was in them. That hope was realized when the first democratic elections were held in April 1994 and were followed by the great celebrations of the fact that at last people of all races could truly call South Africa their home.

The hope that sustains those who struggle in this world to bring about change in the nations extends far beyond our present history.

God's promises are not for this time only but for all eternity. God will keep those promises. They are "trustworthy and true" (Rev. 22:6). No matter how powerful the evil forces of this world may seem to be — whether oppressive authorities or such hostile threats to our humanity as racism, nationalism, sexism, violence, abuse of any kind — they are all finally to be brought under subjection to the rule of Christ (Eph. 1:20f.). In Christ the whole human family is called into unity. So the prayer for the church called to live by this vision must be "that, with the eyes of your heart enlightened, you may know what is the hope to which he has called you, what are the riches of his glorious inheritance among the saints, and what is the immeasurable greatness of his power for us who believe" (Eph. 1:18-19).

PART III

Lenten Liturgical
Bible Studies

Introductory Note

O Lord and Master of my life,
take from me
the spirit of sloth, despair, lust of power and idle talk.
But give rather
the spirit of chastity, humility, patience
and love to your servant.
Yes, O Lord and King, grant to me to see my own sins,
and not to judge my sisters and brothers,
for you are blessed unto ages of ages. Amen.

The Lenten Prayer of St Ephraim the Syrian

Introducing this section with these ancient words, which are prayed by the faithful several times a day during the Lenten period, underscores the link between the WCC assembly theme and the life of the church. The call "Turn to God — Rejoice in Hope" is both a personal call and a call to the community of pilgrims for constant conversion on their faith journey. The three moments which have been identified in the explication of the theme — the memory of God's faithfulness and saving actions, the awareness of the presence of God in daily life, and the hopeful anticipation of the fulfilment of God's promise — are the three moments in the liturgy for the preparation of the eucharist. Living the eucharistic life is living up to the imperatives of the call and the Old Testament jubilee promise on a day-by-day basis. The liturgical calendar is the continual reminder to the church of this call; and the most significant way of remembering this call, both personally and as members of the church, is the period of Great Lent leading to Palm Sunday and Easter.

The biblical passages assigned for the Sundays of the Lenten period prepare the faithful for the celebration of Easter. Since the earliest times of Christianity, what later became known as Great Lent has marked a season of preparation. A central facet of this preparation is an increased and continuous effort of reflection on, confession of and repentance from the sins of the heart, both in thought and through action, including acts of charity and good will. This has also been a period marked by more intensive personal and communal prayer and scripture reading, as well as fasting from food. Great Lent is indeed a welcome opportunity for Christians to set straight their priorities and commitment to the Lord.

Inspired by the ethos of the Lenten period, these liturgical resources offer an approach to the WCC assembly theme through prayer and meditation. The five topics proposed for this "liturgical Bible study" are the five recurring themes of worship during the Lenten period in the Eastern and Oriental Orthodox traditions, which find echoes in all other Christian traditions as well.

What is distinctive about this approach is its structure. It is based on the liturgical form, whose important elements are reading, singing and proclamation, enriched by symbols and rituals. The underlying purpose of all these is to awaken the person, as individual and as member of the Body, from the daily trance of everyday life. They assist us in returning to reality as Christians understand it. In the Christian East, liturgy refers first of all to the eucharist, but in a broader sense also to the various prayer services in the church and to a general doxological stance appropriated by the Christian in daily life.

The biblical readings are drawn from both the Old Testament and the New Testament in order to emphasize the important link between the old and the new, the past and the present: the necessity of transforming memory to reality, a continual reminder of the eucharist. In the tradition of the churches, the biblical texts have been enriched by commentaries, prayers and hymns written on those texts by the church fathers, for example, the Doxology in the Orthodox churches. At the end of each unit a period of reflection and discussion is proposed in order to relate the spiritual experience of the order of this particular worship to life. It is suggested that participants identify a symbol or a ritual that is part of the Lenten worship (icons, rituals of repentance, forgiveness, symbolic acts like the Ash Sunday), and reflect upon its meaning and consequences. We recognize the power of story-telling as a means of confession or repentance, or as an acknowledgment of the presence of God on this spiritual journey.

The five topics covering the period from Lent to Pascha also reflect the elements of the assembly theme: turning to God, rejoicing, hoping. While each topic represents a step in this movement of the assembly theme, each is designed as a liturgical unit which will provide an experience of prayer, reflection and linking of prayer and reflection to the life experiences of the individuals or groups gathered for prayer and study. It is hoped that through this approach, Christians around the world will discover the joy of common understanding and sharing of the Lenten period in anticipation of the Pascha.

As a companion for such a long spiritual journey, an old Armenian hymn eloquently invites each and all to remember the daily need to "turn to God and rejoice in hope":

> I am neither silver in the crucible nor gold tested in fire;
> I am worthless like lead; when exposed I become marred.
> I am neither a rock on the seashore, remaining unmoved against the
>   waves,
> Nor a root of a deep-seated tree, standing unshaken against the winds.
> I am like a wrecked ship, floating to and fro in the sea;
> Or I am like a chaff of hay driven by the wind in autumn.
> Therefore lead me not into temptation,
> you who tempt not those who are
> born of the earth,
> For you are untempted by evil: we are tempted by our selves.
>
> Lenten Hymn, Armenian Liturgy

The Great Return

Recognition of Sin, Reconciliation

Old Testament reading: Isaiah 1:4

From the beginning of the 8th century, long before the birth of Lent, the prophets' message of conversion was addressed with particular emphasis to the entire people who had "forsaken Yahweh and scorned the holy one of Israel".

New Testament reading: Luke 15:11-32

The gospel reading displays one of the fundamental themes of Lent and repentance: that of the return to God. Repentance is depicted as a powerful desire to return to God, a movement of love and trust. The parable of the prodigal son teaches that returning to God is not only a reasonable decision, but above all a deeply felt need on the part of "all that are weary and are carrying heavy burdens" (Matt. 11:28), who abide in the hope that their Father will feed them and so cease to be anxious about their life (Matt. 6:25-32). The forgiveness of the heavenly Father and God's concern for sinners — also expressed in Luke 15 through the parables of the lost sheep and the lost coin — is the call to conversion. In the wider biblical tradition, recognition of one's sins and the psychological consequences of repentance and conversion of the heart are probably most vividly reflected in the case of David, when Nathan intervened with the adulterous king (2 Sam. 11:27-12:15).

Repentance is not a duty to be fulfilled for the sake of God. Repentance is for us. It is the recognition of our unworthiness, the sincere confession of our sins and the complete trust in God's grace: "Father, I have sinned against heaven and before you. I am no longer worthy to be called your son" (Luke 15:21). Today in the ecumenical movement we must probably explore more deeply the potential of a common confession of our mistakes and our sins and of a common return to God as a fundamental element on the way towards a common confession of our faith.

For his part, the Father is not interested in dealing with us in a stern fashion, much less in humiliating us, but rather only in receiving us, embracing us, kissing us and rejoicing with us. All of heaven rejoices over the return of a lost son or daughter. In our relationship with God, God yearns for our return and waits for us. When we return to God, we give him great joy. We do not usually associate joy with repentance. We find it painful to admit our sins, faults and wrongdoing. But we should know that to God repentance is a great moment of joy, because it marks the return of a son or daughter to the loving and waiting Father. It also marks a new personal beginning in living a truer life in communion with the living God.

Meditations

Flee from sin, St Isaac insists; and these three words should be particularly noted. If we are to see God's face reflected within us, the mirror needs to be cleaned. Without repentance there can be no self-knowledge and no discovery of the inward kingdom. When I am told, "Return to yourself: know yourself," it is necessary to inquire: "Which 'self' am I to discover? What *is* my true self?" Psychoanalysis discloses to us one type of "self"; all too often, however, it guides us, not to the "ladder that leads to the kingdom", but to the staircase that goes down to a dank and snake-infested cellar. "Know yourself" means "know yourself as God-sourced, God-rooted; know yourself in God". From the viewpoint of the Orthodox spiritual tradition it should be emphasized that we shall not discover this, our true self "according to the image", except through a death to our false and fallen self. "He who loses his life for my sake shall find it" (Matt. 16:25): only the one who sees this false self for what it is and rejects it will be able to discern his or her true self, the self that God sees. Underlining this distinction between the false self and the true, St Varsanuphius enjoins: "Forget yourself and know yourself."

Bishop Kallistos Ware, UK

Contemporary human beings, whether they have Christian heritage or belong to a people that has not known Christ, have a heightened self-consciousness. We need to take this into consideration and not concentrate only on God, for it is also true that as this heightened self-consciousness developed in modern human beings there developed also a sense of their being powerless by themselves. In these crisscrossing, complex and ever narrower paths of the labyrinth of their conscience, they feel increasingly that there is no spiritual way out, and alone they are lost.

Contemporary human beings, in the sorrow of their solitude and the awareness of their own insufficiency, need more than ever someone else to come to them. From their neighbour they want simplicity and purity, that is, sincerity. This should be strong enough to help them to be steadfast in the difficulties and complexities of their lonely life.

Father Dumitru Staniloae, Romania

Prayer

Let us behold the power of the mystery of salvation!
When the Prodigal Son departed from sin
and returned to his Father's house,
his loving Father came out to meet him and kissed him.
He restored to the Prodigal the signs of his former glory.
Let our lives, then, be worthy of the loving Father,
who has offered the Saviour as sacrifice for us.
Let us pray to him:
as the Prodigal Son I come to you, merciful God;
I have wasted my whole life in a foreign land,
and I have scattered the wealth which you gave me.
Receive me in repentance, O Father,
and have mercy upon me. Amen.

Hymn, Sunday of the Prodigal Son

Hymn

The Great Prokeimenon

Turn not away Thy face from Thy child for I am af - flict - ed. Hear me; speedily draw near un - to my soul and de - li - ver it.

Symbol

Christ praying in the wilderness

Lent is a period of prayer. Praying in the wilderness for forty days, Christ underlines the need for preparation in anticipation of our struggle in the world and the final victory.

Participation in the Joy
of the Lord's Presence

Old Testament reading: Exodus 40:34-36

The ark in the Old Testament is the symbol of the presence of God among his people. The Lord fills with his glory the tent in which the ark of the covenant is placed. Later the tent is replaced by the holy of holies (1 Kings 8:10ff.). People united in the presence of the Lord rejoice in everything they undertake (Deut. 12:18) because in that presence fraternal unity becomes a good and pleasant experience (Ps. 133). From this very image emerges today the challenge to ask all to be together not only in our theological quest and our concerted actions in the world, but above all in prayer: in prayer *for* each other, in prayer *with* each other.

Meditation

We, all Christian nations, adore one Jesus Christ in diverse languages: and we, all the Christians, call ourselves one church of Jesus Christ. We have the same worship, which is expressed in our celebrating the sacrifice of Christ and through which in unison we implore him for salvation of all. That is to say, as the Armenian in his own language implores God for the peace of the world, the well-being of the church, the good conduct of all, temperate weather and the repose of the faithful souls, the Roman Catholic does the same in his language and the Greek Orthodox in his. As Christ is one, the supplication is one...

And when in Spain the Christians pray, the prayer is for me also, because I am a Christian like them; and when it is I that pray in

Cilicia, the prayer is for them also, because they also profess the same faith as I do...

There where the name of God is pronounced, there is our place also. Their prayer is ours, and ours is theirs. It is obvious that as you, in hope and with faith, make offerings to this (your own) church, you are found as being in communion with the church universal. For we do not say, "Have mercy upon and help the Armenian people or the Armenian traveller or the Armenian deceased person." The prayer is not confined to your own. Likewise, the Roman Catholics do not pray only for themselves. We all pray for the church, for the church of all Christians. When you are a (true) believer as a Christian, living or dead, and as the other is the same, you both are encompassed in my prayers.

St Nerses of Lambron, 12th century

New Testament reading: John 1:44-51

A contemporary Coptic monk has said: "My doctor is Jesus Christ, my food is Jesus Christ, my fuel is Jesus Christ." Everything in the church — hymns, prayers, icons, worship, liturgy — unceasingly focuses our attention on Christ. They remind us that the most important duty of the community is to glorify Christ through common prayer and common witness. Therefore, the joy of Philip finding the long awaited Jesus is not fulfilled as an individual feeling but seeks to be shared in a community. So Philip finds Nathanael, and thus they become the nucleus of the community that shares the joy of the presence of the Lord.

Philip's joy announces the joy in front of the risen Christ as expressed in the icon of the Resurrection, in which Adam and Eve in joyful adoration turn to "the true light that enlightens everyone coming into the world" (John 1:9), who steps on his cross to draw them up from the underworld.

Meditation

Nathanael answered: "You are the Son of God! You are the king of Israel!" (John 1:49). See how his soul is filled at once with exceeding joy and he embraces Jesus with his words... See how he leaps and dances with delight! So should we also rejoice, who have been made worthy to know the Son of God — to rejoice not by thought alone but also by our actions. And what must they do who rejoice? Obey him... and do what he wills... When he is hungry, let us feed him; when he is thirsty, let us give him to drink; though you might give him but a cup of water, he receives it; for he loves you, and to one who loves, the offerings of the beloved, though they may be small, appear great.

St John Chrysostom, 4th century

Prayer

Christ our God,
at all times and in every hour,
you are worshipped and glorified in heaven and on earth.
Long in patience, great in mercy and compassion,
you love the righteous and show mercy to the sinners.
You call all to salvation through the promise of good things to come.
Lord, receive our prayers at the present time.
Direct our lives according to your commandments.
Sanctify our souls. Purify our bodies. Set our minds aright.
Cleanse our thoughts,
and deliver us from all sorrow, evil and distress.
Surround us with your holy angels that,
guarded and guided by their host,
we may arrive at the unity of the faith
and the understanding of your ineffable glory.
For you are blessed to the ages of ages. Amen.

Daily Prayer, Great Compline

Hymn

One is Holy, One is Lord, to the Glory of God the Father

Symbol

Armenian cross

The symbol of suffering and hope, the cross is a central element in our spiritual life and a source of inspiration in our Lenten journey (see following page).

Messengers of Hope

Old Testament reading: Isaiah 8:16-18

Messengers of hope were the prophets. Isaiah sees hope hidden from sight, which however will not vanish (cf. Isa. 30:19f.). The faithful and merciful Yahweh is the "hope of Israel" (Jer. 14:8; 17:13f.). Job's hope opens out on the dark night (Job 14:1-6), in spite of certain vague feelings (Job 13:15; 19:25f.). The martyrs' faith begets hope for the resurrection (Dan. 12:1f.; 2 Maccabees 7). Christians today have just begun to reflect on the reality of common martyrs, their contemporary common messengers, who come from different traditions and yet witness together to the same hope for the resurrection, to the same joy at a risen Lord who conquers the principalities and powers of the world.

New Testament reading: Matthew 25:31-46

On the basis of the last judgment this parable reminds us that returning to God entails going to one's neighbour in order to convey the hope inspired by a real presence. This presence is not a moralistic method of life, but an ontological response to the reason of being. It is such a response that made people put their trust in Jesus as a messenger of hope when they carried the paralytic to him (Mark 2:1-12). Offering and receiving in love is the basis of the community of the children of God. Those who are messengers of hope are those who are like the Son of Man who "came to serve, and to give his life as a ransom for many" (Mark 10:45). A messenger of hope is one who responds positively to the call for justice and love — like the steward (Luke 16:1-13), and unlike the rich man who disdained Lazarus in his lifetime (Luke 16:19-31).

Meditations

Men, women and children, profoundly divided as to race, nation, language, manner of life, work, knowledge, honour, fortune... the church re-creates all of them in the Spirit. To all equally she communicates a divine aspect. All receive from her a unique nature which cannot be broken asunder, a nature which no longer permits one to take into consideration the many and profound differences which are their lot. In that way, all are raised up and united in a manner which is truly catholic. In her none is in the least degree separated from the community; all are grounded, so to speak, in one another by the simple and indivisible power of faith... Christ, too, is all in all, he who contains all in himself according to the unique, infinite and all-wise power of his goodness as a centre upon which all lines converge, that the creatures of the one God may not live as strangers or enemies one with another, having no place in common where they may display their love and their peace.

St Maximos the Confessor, 7th century

Christian love is the "possible impossibility" to see Christ in another person, whoever he or she is, and whom God, in his eternal mysterious plan, has decided to introduce into my life, be it only for a few moments, not as an occasion for a "good deed" or an exercise in philanthropy, but as the beginning of an eternal companionship in God's power, which transcends the accidental and the external in origin and intellectual capacity, and reaches the *soul*, the unique and uniquely personal "root" of a human being, truly the part of God in him. If God loves every human being, it is because he alone knows the priceless and absolutely unique treasure, the "soul" or "person" he gave every human being. Christian love then is the participation in that divine knowledge and the gift of that divine love. There is no "impersonal" love because love *is* the wonderful discovery of the "person" in the "human being", of the personal and unique in the common and general. It is the discovery in each human being of that which is "loveable" in him or her, of that which is from God.

Fr Alexander Schmemann, USA

Prayer

The mystery of your coming you did foretell through the prophets of
   Israel,
whom you did choose after Moses;
they spoke through the Holy Spirit in manifold examples;
O Saviour, grant us mercy and forgiveness of our sins.

When the latter years drew near, as the seers had announced,
and you, our Saviour, did arrive in the fullness of time,
you did appear among men having put on the form of a servant;
O Saviour, grant us mercy and forgiveness of our sins.

On the sixth day you did create Adam in the Lordly image;
but he kept not the commandment and was divested of the robe;
wherefore you, O new Adam, did visit the lost one during the sixth
   age;
O Saviour, grant us mercy and forgiveness of our sins.

O temple of light without shadow
and bride-chamber of the ineffable Word,
who did remove the grievous curse on Eve, our first mother;
implore your only-begotten Son,
the mediator of reconciliation with the Father,
that he may be pleased to take away from us all disorder
and to give peace to our souls.

The Divine Liturgy, Armenian

Hymn

The Beatitudes

Russian Orthodox hymn

Re - mem - ber your ser - vants, Lord,

when you come in your king - dom.

1. Bless - ed are the poor in spi - rit;

for theirs is the kingdom of hea - ven.

2. Bless - ed are those who mourn;

for they shall be com - fort - ed.

for   they shall be called   the   chil - dren   of   God.

8. Bless - ed are   those who are perse - cut - ed for   right - eous - ness sake;

for   theirs is the kingdom   of   hea - ven.

9. Bless - ed are   you when the world re - viles you and per - se - cutes you;

and   utters all manner of   evil against you   false - ly   for   my   sake;

Re - joice   and   be   ex - ceed - ing   glad;

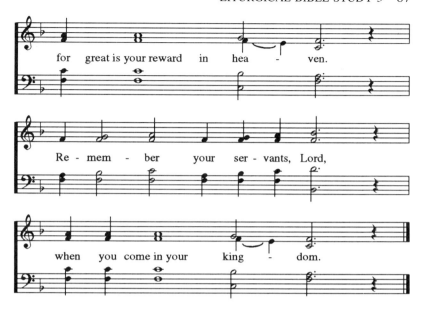

for great is your reward in hea - ven.

Re - mem - ber your ser - vants, Lord,

when you come in your king - dom.

Symbol

Icon of crucifixion

Messengers of hope are all those who, like Mary the mother of Jesus and his beloved disciple John, faithfully remain with Christ and point to him, especially to his suffering and death on the cross, because this is the moment of our own liberation from sin and oppression (see following page).

Call to True Worship

Old Testament reading: Psalm 50

In recalling true worship Psalm 50 is an invitation not to a
meaningless rite but to a fervent prayer of the faithful heart. The peak
of worship is to contemplate Yahweh and live with him (Psalms 63,
84). Christ will institute the perfect form of worship in those poor
hearts who link the meaning of both true justice and hope in singing
the psalms (Matt. 3:1-4). Ezekiel, the prophet-king, while pro-
claiming the ruin of the temple that had been sullied by idolatry, opens
up a new horizon describing the new temple of the new covenant
(Ezek. 37:26f.), which will be the centre of the worship of the faithful
people (Ezek. 40-48)

New Testament reading: John 12:1-18

The adoring affection of the sister of Lazarus anointing Jesus' feet
at Bethany and the reaction of Judas Iscariot open a reflection on what
is the true worship that pleases God. True worship releases emotion
which expresses the will to offer oneself in an unselfish service
(Mary), even under the world's cold and unsympathetic eye (Judas).
Turning to God and rejoicing in hope are related to worship as either
an individual act of devotion or as a communal expression of faith in
the one who comes in the name of the Lord. The triumphal entry into
Jerusalem with its "Hosannas!" has only the external characteristics of
worship. In true worship, "Hosanna" is the rediscovery of peace and
thirst for God.

True worship ends by transforming memory to reality through the
eucharist (Matt. 26:17-30). The long memorial prayer in the eucharis

tic service brings the past into our present, into our own history. Thus the whole history of salvation becomes our history.

The meeting with the Lord in the eucharist, where we present ourselves in repentance, humility and trust, is an ever-renewing encounter which transforms and transfigures our lives. Because of this encounter we can sing "We have seen the true light!".

During the eucharist the Holy Spirit projects the full image of the kingdom into history, onto the church gathered together. Here lies the source of our real hope. In the eucharist we become aware of the past, we understand better our condition, we are informed about realities to come. We are renewed to continue our struggle, a struggle for repentance and witness to the world.

Meditations

When the saints become perfect, they enter into communion with God in the outpouring of love for him and their fellow human persons. The saints themselves seek this sign of their union with God: that is, that they have the passionate desire to be merciful to their neighbour. This is what our monastic fathers and mothers did when growing in the perfection and likeness of God, always receiving in themselves the fullness of life in Christ... Let it further be said that those who idolatrously love this world cannot realize love for their fellow human persons. For when one obtains love, the person is, together with it, clothed in God.

St Isaac the Syrian, 7th century

The Orthodox tradition is, in fact, soaked in the idea of repentance. It affirms that a Christian must constantly repent. All the fasts, vigils, prayers and other ascetic disciplines are special occasions for intense repentance. The prayers in the Great Lent constantly remind the people to repent and be converted. In the monastic tradition, the monks understood their whole life as dedicated to prayer and repentance. The difference in the Eastern tradition, however, is that, according to the liturgical texts, it is always the mother church who calls her children to repentance, to turn to the Father, the source of all life. The mother is intensely interceding on behalf of all her children. Inspired by the Spirit, the church participates in the high priestly prayer of Christ, by offering the whole creation through Christ to the

Father and rendering thanks for all the gifts of God. This intercession of the people of God as one body, the Body of Christ, and the call for repentance made by the church to her children cannot be reduced to easily analyzable rational propositions. It is to be perceived rather as a never-ceasing movement of the whole creation oriented to the source of light, illumined and transfigured by the ineffable glory of the triune God.

Fr K.M. George, India

Prayer

Master and Lord Almighty,
look down from heaven upon your church,
and upon all your people, and all your flocks,
and save all of us your unworthy servants,
the creatures of your fold;
grant to us your peace, and your love, and your help;
send down upon us the gifts of your most Holy Spirit,
that, in a pure heart, and with a good conscience,
we may salute one another with a holy kiss,
not in hypocrisy, but blameless and unspotted,
in one spirit, in the bond of peace and of love,
one body and one spirit, in one faith,
as we have also been called in one hope of our calling,
that we may all of us arrive at the divine and boundless affection,
in Christ Jesus, our Lord,
with whom you are blessed. Amen.

Prayer from the Liturgy of St Mark

Hymn

O gladsome light

Byzantine Chant

O Glad-some Light of the ho-ly glo — ry of the

im-mor-tal Fa — ther, heav — en-ly, ho — ly,

bless ed, Je - sus Christ! Now that we have come to the

set-ting of the sun and be-hold the light of eve - ning,

we praise God: Fa-ther, Son, and Ho-ly Spir - it.

For meet it is at all times to wor-ship Thee with

voic — es of praise, O Son of God and

Giv — er of Life!

There - fore all the world doth glo - ri - fy Thee.

Symbol

Mary at the feet of Jesus (John 12:3-8)

Cross, Resurrection, Pentecost

The Hope

Old Testament reading: Isaiah 52:13

The prophets in their time looked forward in anticipation to the advent of the Messiah (Isa. 52:13-53:12; Zech. 12:8-14). Another meaningful passage for our theme could be taken from Hosea, who not only announces the Messiah but also calls us to return to him in order to be healed, to live and experience true joy: "Come, let us return to the Lord; for it is he who has torn, and he will heal us; he has struck down, and he will bind us up. After two days he will revive us; on the third day he will raise us up, that we may live before him" (6:1-2).

New Testament reading: Mark 8:34-39

Christian hope passes through the experience of the cross (Mark 8:34-39; Mark 10:32-45). This is the return from death to joy of the life-giving Christ (John 1:1-17; Mark 16:2-8), as the result of the uniting gift of the Holy Spirit, who is everywhere and fills everything, unlike the unhappy effect of discordant voices of humankind (John 7:37-52; 8:12).

This part represents the zenith of the experience of Christian life as a life of continual repentance and joy lived in the church throughout the year through the liturgical calendar, and then lived in a compact way during the Lenten period.

Prayer

He whom none may touch is seized;
He who looses Adam and Eve from the curse is bound.
He who tries the hearts and inner thoughts of humanity
    is unjustly brought to trial;
He who closed the abyss is shut in prison.
He before whom the powers of heaven stand with trembling
    stands before Pilate;
The Creator is struck by the hand of his creature.
He who comes to judge the living and the dead
    is condemned to the Cross;
The Destroyer of hell is enclosed in a tomb.
O you, who endured all of these things,
in your tender love,
who has saved all humankind from the curse,
O longsuffering Lord, glory to you.

From Vespers on Great Friday

Note: "Adam" here signifies male and female humanity, "Eve" is implied.
Nevertheless, her name was added for pastoral reasons.

Meditations

Wouldst thou learn thy Lord's meaning in this thing? Learn it well: Love was his meaning. Who showed it thee? Love. What showed he thee? Love. Wherefore showed it he? For Love. Hold thou therein and thou shalt learn and know more in the same. But thou shalt never know nor learn therein other thing without end...

Julian of Norwich, UK

From its very beginning Christianity has been the proclamation of joy, of the only possible joy on earth... Without the proclamation of this joy Christianity is incomprehensible. It is only as joy that the church was victorious in the world and it lost the world when it lost the joy... "For behold, I bring you tidings of great joy..." — thus begins the gospel, and its end is: "And they worshipped him and returned to

Jerusalem with great joy…" (Luke 2:10; 24:52). And we must recover the meaning of this great joy.

Fr Alexander Schmemann, USA

It is only by being a prisoner for religious convictions in a Soviet camp that one can really understand the mystery of the fall of the first man, the mystical meaning of the redemption of all creation and the great victory of Christ over the forces of evil. It is only when we suffer for the ideals of the holy gospel that we can realize our sinful infirmity and our unworthiness in comparison with the great martyrs of the first Christian church. Only then can we grasp the absolute necessity for profound meekness and humility, without which we cannot be saved; only then can we begin to discern the passing image of the seen, and the eternal life of the Unseen.

On Easter Day all of us who were imprisoned for religious convictions were united in the one joy of Christ. We were all taken into one feeling, into one spiritual triumph, glorifying the one eternal God. There was no solemn paschal service with the ringing of church bells, no possibility in our camp to gather for worship, to dress up for the festival, to prepare Easter dishes. On the contrary, there was even more work and more interference than usual. All the prisoners here for religious convictions, whatever their denomination, were surrounded by more spying, by more threats from the secret police.

Yet Easter was there: great, holy, spiritual, unforgettable. It was blessed by the presence of our risen God among us — blessed by the silent Siberian stars and by our sorrows. How our hearts beat joyfully in communion with the great resurrection! Death is conquered, fear no more, an eternal Easter is given to us! Full of this marvellous Easter, we send you from our prison camp the victorious and joyful tidings: Christ is risen!

(Letter from a Soviet concentration camp,
cited by Bishop Kallistos Ware)

Prayer

Is there anyone who is devout and a lover of God?
Come, and receive this bright, this beautiful feast of feasts!
Is there anyone who is a wise servant?
Rejoice, as you enter into the joy of your Lord!
Is there anyone who is weary from fasting?
Come, and receive your reward!
Is there anyone who has laboured from the first hour?
Accept today your fair wages!
Is there anyone who came after the third hour?
Have no doubts, for nothing is being held back!
Is there anyone who delayed until the ninth hour?
Come forward, without any hesitation!
Is there anyone who came up only at the eleventh hour?
Do not be afraid because of your lateness!

For the honour and generosity of the Master is unsurpassed.
He accepts the last as well as the first,
he gives rest to the eleventh-hour arrival as well as to the
     one who laboured from the first;
he is as merciful to the former as he is gracious to the latter;
he shows his generosity to the one, and his kindness to the
     other;
he honours the deed and commends the purpose.

Therefore, enter all of you into the joy of your Lord!
Both first and last, receive the reward;
rich and poor, dance and sing together;
continent and dissolute, honour this day;
fasters and non-fasters, enjoy a feast today.
The table is filled, and everyone should share in the luxury;
the calf is fatted, and no one must go away hungry.

Come, one and all, and receive the banquet of faith!
Come, one and all, and receive the riches of loving-kindness!
No one must lament his poverty,
for a kingdom belonging to all has appeared;
no one must despair over his failings,
for forgiveness has sprung up from the grave;
no one must fear death,
for the death of the Saviour has set us all free.

By being held in its power he extinguished it,
and by descending into Hades he made Hades a captive.
He embittered it when it tasted his flesh.
And in anticipation of this, Isaiah exclaimed:
"Hades was in an uproar, meeting you below."

It was in an uproar, for it was wiped out;
it was in an uproar, for it was mocked;
it was in an uproar, for it was vanquished;
it was in an uproar, for it was bound in chains.
It took a body, and met up with God;
it took earth, and came face to face with heaven;
it took what it saw, and was struck down by what it did
    not see.

O death, where is your sting?
O Hades, where is your victory?

Christ is risen, and you are laid low;
Christ is risen, and the demons are struck down;
Christ is risen, and the angels rejoice;
Christ is risen, and life is abundant and free;
Christ is risen, and there are no dead left in the tombs!
For Christ, when he has raised from the dead, became the
    first fruits of those who have fallen asleep.
Glory to him! and power, now and always and unto ages of ages.
Amen.

St John Chrysostom, 4th century

Hymn

Christ is risen

Alex. Podoleanu: Romania

Symbol

The icon of resurrection

Acknowledgments

Special thanks go to Musimbi Kanyoro for her preparation of the Bible studies, to Pauline Webb for her preparation of the meditations, and to Terry MacArthur for putting the music on computer.

We are also grateful to the following persons who contributed to the production of the Bible studies, meditations and liturgical resources: Kamol Arayaprateep, Khushnud Azariah, Tom Best, Francis Cais SDB, Neville Callam, Saramma Eapen, Araceli Ezzati, Glynthea Finger, Kyriaki FitzGerald, Irene Foulkes, Jean Fountilous, Crescencia Gabijan, Leonido Gaede, Olga Ganaba, Virginia Gcabashe, Peter Gramatikov, Athanasios Hatzopoulos, Dagmar Heller, Nangula Kathindi, Georges Lemopoulos, Peter Lodberg, George Malebe, Nadeje Mandysova, Carolyn McComish, John Neill, Jacques Nicole, Amos Omodunbi, Ofelia Ortega, Teny Pirri-Simonian, Konrad Raiser, Kathy Reeves, Raquel Rodriguez, Horace Russell, Jakub Santoya, Shahan Sarkissian, Ninevi Seddoh, Turid Karlsen Seim, Kenneth Thomas, Kristine Thompson, George Tinker, Joanna Udal, Marlin VanElderen, Petros Vassiliadis, Angelique Walker-Smith, Elizabeth Welch and Yeow Choo Lak.

Photos

Page 4: Squatters along the coastal highway, Ipanima, Brazil (WCC/Peter Williams)

Page 11: A gypsy woman and her child along the Kurfürstendamm, Berlin (WCC/Wolf Kutnahorsky)

Page 20: Wat Than rehabilitation centre, Phnom Penh, Cambodia (WCC/Peter Williams)

Page 26: Street scene in New York City (WCC/Jean-Claude Lejeune)

Page 32: Eucharistic liturgy in the Orthodox cathedral of Iasi, Romania (WCC/ Peter Williams)

Page 38: The Episcopal cathedral in Yambio, Western Equatoria province, Sudan (WCC/Peter Williams)

Page 42: Greek Orthodox church, Damascus, Syria (WCC/Peter Williams)

Page 75: Christ praying in the wilderness (John Matusiak, reprinted from Thomas Hopko, *The Orthodox Faith. Vol. IV: Spirituality*, New York, OCA, 1976)

Page 80: Traditional Armenian cross, Holy Etchmiadzin (WCC/Peter Williams)

Page 88: Orthodox icon of the crucifixion (WCC)

Page 93: Mary at the feet of Jesus (John Matusiak, reprinted from Hopko)

Page 100: Byzantine icon of the resurrection (WCC)